# 7 Steps to Sales Force Transformation

# 7 Steps to Sales Force Transformation

## Driving Sustainable Change in Your Organization

*Warren Shiver*
*and*
*Michael Perla*

First published 2016 by
PALGRAVE MACMILLAN

The authors have asserted their rights to be identified as the authors of this work in accordance with the Copyright, Designs and Patents Act 1988.

Palgrave Macmillan in the UK is an imprint of Macmillan Publishers Limited, registered in England, company number 785998, of Houndmills, Basingstoke, Hampshire, RG21 6XS.

Palgrave Macmillan in the US is a division of Nature America, Inc., One New York Plaza, Suite 4500, New York, NY 10004-1562.

Palgrave Macmillan is the global academic imprint of the above companies and has companies and representatives throughout the world.

Hardback ISBN: 978–1–137–54804–7
E-PUB ISBN: 978–1–137–54806–1
E-PDF ISBN: 978–1–137–54805–4
DOI: 10.1057/9781137548054

Distribution in the UK, Europe and the rest of the world is by Palgrave Macmillan®, a division of Macmillan Publishers Limited, registered in England, company number 785998, of Houndmills, Basingstoke, Hampshire RG21 6XS.

Library of Congress Cataloging-in-Publication Data

Shiver, Warren.
    7 steps to sales force transformation : driving sustainable change in your organization / Warren Shiver, Michael Perla.
        pages cm
    Includes index.
        ISBN 978–1–137–54804–7 (alk. paper)
        1. Sales management. 2. Organizational change. I. Perla, Michael. II. Title. III. Title: Seven steps to sales force transformation.

HF5438.4.S4935 2015
658.8′102—dc23                                                    2015026334

A catalogue record for the book is available from the British Library.

Printed in the United States of America.

# Contents

# Figures

# Tables

# Acknowledgments

This book is not only a collaborative effort between the authors but also involved many others in different capacities.

We have the pleasure of working with a wonderfully talented team at Symmetrics Group, all of whom have contributed to our thinking and to the client experiences that have shaped this book. Specifically, we thank Rachel Cavallo and David Szen for their contributions on change management and sales leadership and their help as a sounding board during this project.

Thank you to our writer, Louis Greenstein, who pushed us to continually share our experiences and lessons learned through stories, to John Willig of Literary Services Inc. who believed in our project and to Laurie Harting and the team at Palgrave Macmillan, who brought this book to reality.

We greatly appreciate our clients and the executives who willingly shared their time, experiences, and lessons learned. They include Allison Montgomery, Bruce Hembree, Carl Strenger, Chris Donato, Lynn Duclos, David Fulham, David Mears, David Pyle, David Roche, Don Perry, Eileen Martinson, Everett Hill, Gus Halas, J. D. Walker, Jill Cady, Jim Dougherty, Jim Neve, Ken Revenaugh, Ketan Desai, Kyle Bowker, Larry Stack, Lindsey Nelson, Lisa Fiondella, Lisa Redkop, Lou Hutchinson, Mark Weiner, Marty Fagan, Michael Hargis, Michael Woodard, Michael Conway, Mike Dickerson, Paul Duval, Ralph Chauvin, Robert Fox, Robert McDowell, Scott David, Steve

Meirink, Steve Young, Stephen Powell, Tom Martin, Vince Corica, and Warwick Johnston.

Thank you also to Jennifer Hale, Mark Donnolo, Mark Hawn, Mo Bunnell, David Hamme, David Mast, Tom Martin, and Michael Merlin for their support of this project and of the authors and our firm for many years.

We would also like to thank our families for supporting our professional passion and the late nights and weekends we spent with this project. Thank you to Paige, Avery, and Morgan Shiver, and to Kirsten, Nicholas, and Brooke Perla.

We are passionate about the selling profession and have thoroughly enjoyed capturing many experiences from sales and business leaders. Our hope is that this book will serve as a guide to help you, the readers, improve your sales performance: as an individual, in your team, and in your organization.

Good reading and good selling.

# Introduction

We knew within the first ten minutes that Paul Duval was an executive we wanted to work with on the transformation of his company's sales force. We were sitting at a small, round conference table in Paul's neatly organized corner office in a one-story office park in northwest Atlanta on a rainy afternoon in late July. Paul was senior vice president (SVP) of sales for the garden division of Central Garden & Pet, a leading provider of branded lawn and garden products to large national retailers, such as Home Depot, Lowe's, and Walmart, as well as to regional chains and small local stores. He had been working for Central for about three years.

Rarely had we met a sales leader who could so succinctly describe his vision for a team. Over the course of our 60-minute initial meeting, we discussed Central's current metrics, feedback from top customers, and Paul's previous experience transforming sales organizations as an executive with the Scotts Company. He also described how Central was on the verge of sweeping change: the company's new CEO, Gus Halas, was a perfect example of a "change agent." Gus, whose background included several corporate turnarounds, brought a sharp focus on operational and financial improvement to Central. Prior to Gus's arrival, the organization had grown—through more than 40 acquisitions—to a "portfolio of companies," as Paul described it. Gus's goal was to focus on manufacturing, supply chain, shipping, tracking, and operational improvements to transform Central into a "portfolio of brands."

Paul recognized that for Gus's overhaul of Central to be successful and sustainable, the sales force also needed to change from its current focus on transactional selling to a more consultative approach, one that could bring category and consumer insights to the company's retailer customers through an ongoing dialogue aligned to the retailers' priorities, long-term strategies, and innovations. But Paul was wise enough to know that the need for sales force transformation might not be as evident to the new CEO or to the rest of the executive team as it was to him. While Central was teeing up to fundamentally change how products were manufactured, shipped, and tracked, those outside of the sales department might have assumed that all sales had to do was "get out there and sell." But Paul knew he'd need to "sell" sales force transformation to Gus and the executive team. Therefore, he'd need to treat the vision and initial stages of obtaining executive buy-in like an internal sales campaign. Another thing Paul knew was that, as he put it, "I couldn't run the business while making substantial changes," which is a typical comment from a sales leader who must balance "making the number" today with driving changes that will equip the sales team for success going forward.

After that initial meeting in July, we spent six weeks collaborating on a vision and a case for sales force transformation. This included riding along with sales representatives and a plant tour in Madison, Georgia. There's no substitute for experiencing a day in the life of a sales rep and speaking directly with customers. With an overall assessment, first-hand interviews, and plenty of exposure to sales and customer conversations, we built a case for sales force transformation, and we charted an initial roadmap for Paul and his team.

A couple of weeks later, as I (Warren) was navigating my way through security and crowds at New York's LaGuardia airport, my phone rang. It was Paul calling to tell me that his internal sales campaign had been successful and that he'd received approval from Gus to launch a transformation of the sales team. Having heard Paul's pitch, Gus and the executive team agreed and supported the case for transformation that was built around the need to align the sales team with the organizational changes. This approval launched a major effort focused on sales and marketing and connected with Central's overall business transformation. The work we at Symmetrics Group did in helping Central to transform its sales team was a great professional experience for the authors and one that we'll draw on throughout this book, as our direct experience with Central (supported by interviews with Paul, Gus, and others) has informed our approach to sales force transformation. Over the years, we have helped a number of sales forces, both large and small, transform the way they sell. For this book we interviewed sales leaders with whom we have worked as well as others we have come to admire. We also conducted an extensive survey of sales professionals; the results confirmed what we've learned along the way and highlighted some obvious miscalculations organizations make when approaching sales force transformation. For example, while there is general agreement that the HR department must be involved in any significant sales force transformation, fewer than half our survey respondents (47.6 percent) reported that HR was actually involved in theirs. In our research we found a number of similar discrepancies that likely undermined what might otherwise have been successful transformation initiatives. While every organization is different (which is why there is no recipe for sales force transformation), successful initiatives tend to have a number of things in common. In this book, we take a closer look at them.

In chapter 1, "The Transformation Dilemma," we'll discuss the challenge of effecting sustained change and the question of whether your sales organization is ready for transformation (or if all it needs is a tweak). In chapter 2, "The Levers of Sales Transformation," we'll explore a number of transformation fundamentals including how to perform an inside-out/outside-in analysis, how to align sales transformation efforts with other departments as an organization undergoes significant change, how to enable and measure transformation, and how to communicate about it. Chapter 3, "Building the Foundation and Vision of the Future," will walk you through the drivers that can spark the need for a sales transformation and how to create a vision tailored to the unique needs and specific goals of your organization. Chapter 4, "Treating Your Sales Transformation Like an Internal Sale," will help you clarify your change strategy and sell it to senior management, as Paul Duval did at Central Garden & Pet. Chapter 5,

"Building Your Sales Transformation Roadmap," introduces a multistep process involving the formulation of strategy and structure, processes and tools, enablement and people, and metrics and management—all keys to a successful transformation initiative. Chapter 6, "Launching Your Sales Transformation," is about how to get started deploying your initiative—whether to roll it out as a comprehensive program or as a pilot, depending on factors such as budget, time, the size of your organization, and the degree of executive buy-in. Chapter 7, "Key Barriers and Considerations for Implementation," captures the significant "lessons learned" when rolling out a sales force transformation. Chapter 8, "Extending Your Sales Transformation to Business Partners, Suppliers, and Customers," covers the oft-forgotten discipline of including these critical third parties in your transformation initiative. In chapter 9, "Sustaining Your Transformation," we explain why it's critical to sustain your transformation through leadership, training, communications, management tools, hiring, onboarding, and beyond. After all, you can't expect the results to sustain themselves. And in chapter 10, "Sales Transformations in the Future," we examine current trends that will impact your ability to lead and drive change in sales forces going forward.

One significant challenge for sales leaders seeking to transform their sales organization is time. The average tenure of a chief sales officer is just 18 months. So, if the sales leaders want to make a difference, speed is essential. The good news, according to our survey of sales leaders, is that in about 66 percent of successful transformations, positive results were seen in one year or less.

In our experience, there is no prescribed methodology, no off-the-shelf solution for managing a successful sales force transformation. You won't learn how to do it at a conference, in a webinar, or from a DVD. Let's face it: if there were a tried and true method, you'd have heard about it by now. There are, however, guidelines and best practices to help an organization navigate its way through a successful transformation. That's what you'll find in this book. Through our original quantitative research, our own experiences transforming sales organizations, and the lessons learned by a host of sales professionals we interviewed, you will begin to understand how to transform your sales force. If your organization is large like Central, you may need outside help. But it's not the sort of initiative you can simply turn over to a vendor. That's why you need this book. And if your organization is small, you will find that sales force transformation is challenging and time-consuming—yet necessary if the organization is to survive. In that case, you also need this book!

# CHAPTER 1

# The Transformation Dilemma

We were in an office tower, meeting with a sales executive at a global hospitality company with a sales force comprising thousands of individuals worldwide. Like most global hospitality companies, the sales organization included two kinds of teams: corporate teams that pursued contracts with regional and global companies and "on property" sales teams that worked on-site at individual hotels to increase business for their properties. The executive we were talking with, Jane (not her real name), needed these two historically siloed groups—each with its own metrics, goals, and processes—to work together to better serve corporate customers. Jane's goal was to create a "common sales language" to improve collaboration and communications. In a far-reaching conversation about her vision and the processes she wanted to drive, we turned to Jane and asked, "Do you think your sales team will buy in and adopt these changes?"

Jane shrugged. "Well, sure," she said. "They'll go along with this because they want to be world-class salespeople." On the surface, her response made perfect sense. After all, salespeople and their leaders are typically motivated by competition, recognition, and winning; so if you want them to change, just show them how much more success, recognition, or compensation they can achieve by taking a new approach. They'll fall in line, right?

Unfortunately, it's not so simple. Even when the need for transformation is evident, salespeople are generally resistant to change. Many salespeople have ingrained habits that have brought them at least some level of success or they would have found a different profession. There's a lot at stake. Selling is a very transparent activity; it's clear how you are performing and the numbers "don't lie." For salespeople, any change distracts them from their ultimate goal: driving sales and exceeding their quota. As a manager, you also need to determine if there is a "will" or "skill" issue in terms of changing. For the former, is there a motivation to change? For the latter, is the change beyond the skills and capabilities of the salespeople? Finally, you must consider the overall structure of the change and what it means for the company.

In most companies, everyone expects growth—investors, executives, leaders, customers, and employees. Most people want to work for and with growing organizations. In general, growth is usually seen as positive—more opportunity, more money, more options. The upside of successfully transforming a sales organization can be significant:

- increased revenue
- reduced cost of sales
- increased lead conversion rates
- improved sales and share of wallet with existing high-potential customers

But the downside can be daunting. According to a McKinsey study, 75 percent of companies that attempted to transform to a solutions-selling approach failed to produce a return on their investment in transformation.[1] The potential rewards are significant, but the road to success is paved with failures. Often, the root of the failure is that salespeople are reluctant to change, even when the need to change appears obvious.

Welcome to the transformation dilemma.

## What Is Sales Force Transformation?

We define sales force transformation as a *holistic* and *multidimensional* program, one that touches on every part of the organization, not just sales, and that fundamentally changes the way a sales force sells. Typically, these transformations take more than a year and require a significant investment of time, money, and other resources.

If a lamp goes dark, you change a light bulb; if a house lacks electricity, and you wire it from top to bottom—*that's* a transformation. In that context, we look at transformation as a sustained and measurable program that requires a series of changes. Change, as we see it, is a subset and a critical component of transformation. If you switch jobs, you have made a change. But let's say you quit your job, move to France, and enroll in culinary school, and then launch a new career as a chef. That's not just a change; it's a transformation (or potentially a midlife crisis, but that topic is covered extensively by other books and authors).

What is sales transformation? It's *change* writ large.

## Why Sales Force Transformation Is a Challenge

Change is hard. We all know that. But some changes are harder than others; they're bigger and scarier. Say you work in finance or accounting or in a service field such as healthcare. Those industries are always changing in response to government regulations, local policies, developments in technology and other factors. If you're an accountant and the Internal Revenue Service (IRS) or Financial Accounting Standards Board (FASB) issues a new rule, you do what it takes to adapt to it. You read up on it, maybe take a class, and/or consult the IRS. It takes time and energy, and it may cause some stress. But you get it done because there is no other option.

Sales, however, is different. Salespeople, by and large, are independent and entrepreneurial. Most will tell you that they don't just sell their products; they sell themselves. That's where the dilemma begins. If you try to change people who are out there selling themselves day in and day out, you will likely learn that most salespeople are intrinsically resistant to change. Research has shown that salespeople resist change they perceive to be related to "painful" outcomes, such as reduced pay, lower job satisfaction, and an increase in workload.[2] In some ways, salespeople have a unique role in managing competing commitments to their company and to the servicing of their customers. In our experience, many salespeople who are exceeding their quotas get a pass when it comes to change. Very few sales leaders will make an example out of a top-performing salesperson who doesn't change. For an example of trying to change the sales force, let's look back at Central Garden & Pet that we described in the introduction.

In that case—and in others we have seen—sales forces are called upon to change the fundamentals of how they sell. That can be scary. And what can be even scarier is that when a sales organization successfully transforms, the rest of the business might not keep up. Unfortunately, this happened at Central and led to a disappointing Pyrrhic victory while providing a wealth of valuable lessons, as we'll see. As we point out throughout the book, sales transformation might not equal business transformation. You could optimize the sales organization from strategy to leadership to sales force effectiveness, and the company could still have performance challenges. Sales transformation will not solve all the supply chain or operational issues in a company. Like many case studies from such well-known business books as *In Search of Excellence*,[3] *Built to Last*,[4] or *Good to Great*,[5] it's very hard to find an enduring company that is always a top performer and doesn't succumb to a business cycle or temporary business issues. Central Garden & Pet is one of those cases.

After the sales organization went through a transformation, sales increased by 22 percent for the company's largest sales team. Unfortunately, this success was not sustained due to some of the challenges in Central's supply chain and general business operations. Even though the company's long-term business results were not in the top quartile after we wound down our efforts, the lessons and insights from its sales transformation are worth learning from and exploring. Frank Cespedes, in his wonderful book, *Aligning Strategy and Sales: The Choice, Systems, and Behaviors that Drive Effective Selling*, makes the point very well: "Management writers who don't acknowledge their own mistakes either are perfect (very unlikely), have never managed (common), or are incapable of learning because business and selling are for big stretches about learning (as efficiently and effectively as possible) from inevitable mistakes."[6]

Many successful salespeople will tell you that they don't need to change; they've found an approach that's working (especially if they're hitting their numbers), and adopting new corporate or institutional approaches runs against their nature. For them, to paraphrase Ronald Reagan, the eight most feared words in the English language are: "I'm from corporate, and I'm here to help." This resistance is compounded by the fact that when we talk about sales force transformation, we mean sweeping, dramatic change that can feel disruptive and may carry a degree of risk, both for the individual and for the company.

Often, even when people want to change and see a good reason for it, it's a daunting task with a high failure rate. For example, think about all the people you know who should lose weight, quit smoking, or make other significant lifestyle changes. In most cases, they know what they're supposed to do, and they have good motivations for doing it, but—well, change is hard.

In a recent survey, a food company found that of people who diet regularly, two out of five quit within the first seven days, one out of five last a month, and the same number—just 20 percent—make it to the three-month mark.[7] Sticking with a transformative change—whether it's the way you eat or the way you sell—takes commitment and a number of supporting factors, which we'll outline in this book. The good news is that in our research, we found that 80 percent of organizations that successfully execute a sales force transformation typically see meaningful results in the first year. The challenge, like a diet, is to extend and sustain those gains beyond the initial lift. However, these gains come at a significant cost of time, money, resources, and leadership commitment.

So, before you dive into a transformation effort, you want to be sure transformation is what your sales organization actually needs, rather than smaller, incremental changes (tweaks). The lessons contained in this book will help you step through either a big-T Transformation or a small-t tweak. But before we go any further, let's talk a little about the difference between the two.

## *Transform versus Tweak*

Prior to starting up Symmetrics Group, we worked for a number of major training, sales, and software firms where we developed our expertise in sales effectiveness. We've found recently that many sales training companies use the word "transformation" when they're really only talking about tweaking the existing organization, mostly through training, not holistic transformation. Depending on your case for change and the gap between your capabilities and desired results, rolling out sales training or a new tool might be the perfect solution. Training could effect the change you need. Training could also prepare a sales force for an eventual transformation initiative or reinforce a transformation you have recently undergone. But as we'll soon see, training is not transformation.

A recent sales training bestseller, *The Challenger Sale*[8] by Matthew Dixon and Brent Adamson of The Corporate Executive Board, describes research showing that the buying process has fundamentally changed thanks to the knowledge and resources now available to buyers (mainly due to the Internet). It goes on to suggest that in many situations, sellers must add value above and beyond their products or services by employing a consultative selling approach where they bring insights to their customers and "challenge" or "reframe" the customer's perception of a problem or opportunity. In an article in the *Harvard Business Review* that summarizes the need for this approach, the authors state, "Getting the Challenger approach right requires organizational capabilities as well as individual skills."[9] To us, this is the essential but often overlooked key point, as many organizations, like our dieters, only focus on one thing and look for a short-term fix, in this case running a two- or three-day sales training workshop to roll out a new sales technique. Sometimes a tweak (delivered through training or a new tool) is all a sales force needs; other times, a full-bore transformation is in order. Transforming a sales organization to consistently deliver insights requires new value propositions, case studies and collateral from the marketing department, new competencies, skill development, recruiting profiles from HR, and alignment with operations to refine products and services. A theme that runs through our experience and this book is that successful sales transformations must involve other functional areas of the business.

We've spoken with sales leaders who think their organizations need to transform, when all that is required is a tweak. This tweak or change may lead to transformation, or it might not. For example, a sales leader at a major health care insurance company told independent sales consultant and former IBM sales enablement manager Don Perry that the company's problem was that it wasn't getting enough sales and that it was looking to "transform our sales capability to deliver our numbers." But when Don visited the company's call center, he was surprised by what he observed: In call after call, the rep had the customer in the bag. The sale was virtually made; the only thing left was the close. Then the salesperson would say, "I have to call you back later. We'll finish this discussion." The reps got off the phone in fewer than 14 minutes. Don was astonished and told us, "All they had to do was stay on the phone for a couple more minutes to close the sale!"

Don asked around. He soon learned that the call center's top performer was completing calls in 14 minutes or less. Yet, the top performer had no sales. Turns out, performance was measured by how quickly sales reps could make it through the script, not by sales volume—a classic misalignment of metrics. Don returned to the sales leader and suggested that the sales calls should be extended by about two minutes with a couple of small script changes, and he asked if he could test it out with one of the department's poorest performers. "I took a person about to be fired, gave them a script and they went from last place to first place in three days!" he told us. That easy-to-close gap (the enhanced call script) not only positioned the call center for better sales, but it made the company more attentive to Don's ideas for improvements in other areas (an ultimate sales transformation).

In fact, there are many ways to change and improve a sales organization that stop short of transformation. In a simplified continuum of change that companies embark on when they aim to improve their sales effectiveness (which usually means driving specific metrics and results in an effort to attack weaknesses or seize opportunities that have been clearly identified), the process progresses from sales training to the implementation of a tool or new process to new sales leadership/ teams and then to sales transformation. In reality, most plans are a combination of these elements.

As a leader in your organization, you must determine up-front if you need transformation or just an incremental improvement. Often this process begins with an understanding of where you are today and where you want to be—a topic that we'll discuss in coming chapters. But for now, let's walk through an initial exercise to get a sense of whether your sales force needs a transformation or a tweak.

### *Qualifying Your Transformation*

Though the words "change" and "transformation" are sometimes used interchangeably, not all change rises to the level of transformation. Before we describe a few examples of sales force transformations we've seen (successful as well as unsuccessful) here are four simple questions to help determine whether your organization needs a sales force transformation or just a tweak. Think of this exercise as a way to qualify your sales force for transformation the way marketing qualifies a lead or the way a salesperson qualifies a prospect. To do this, take a few moments to consider the biggest single issue your sales force faces—the issue that inspired you to pick up a book about sales force transformation. Write it down. Then ask yourself:

1. *Is the solution to this challenge mostly addressable by training?* As mentioned, one of the most common misperceptions we've seen is the notion that training equals transformation. Sometimes transformation requires training, but training per se is not transformation. If your organization provides sales training after not having provided it, that's a change, but it's not a transformation. Nor is training-session feedback transformation. "Smile sheets" may be a fine way to assess training and for trainers to get constructive criticism from trainees. They may help trainers to become more effective, which is certainly a good thing. But training alone will

not transform a sales organization. For example, we worked with one client company that trained all of its sellers on consultative selling behaviors, but didn't change the processes, metrics, or management cadence to reinforce the new behaviors. The training got rave reviews, but it was treated as an isolated event. Subsequently, the sales organization didn't transform, and the training was soon forgotten. If your sales force needs vital product information, if it needs to embrace new rules or regulations, or if you are seeking incremental sales growth in your current markets with your current offerings, you probably need to roll out training, not transformation. But if you need to change the fundamentals of how your sales force sells—and you want that change to stick—you're likely looking at transformation.

2. *Will technology alone help you meet the challenge?* As with training, your organization's transformation initiative may require new tools and systems, but adding a CRM tool or even an entire IT group are not sales transformations per se. At best, sales-oriented systems help to automate and enable processes, but they must be accompanied by many other elements such as manager reinforcement, coaching, metrics, and training to drive user adoption and, ultimately, the desired ROI. Even though CRM as a technology is approaching its third decade, we still see companies confuse the implementation of CRM with sales transformation. The technology may be necessary for a sales transformation, but it's rarely sufficient on its own. If you are satisfied with your current levels of sales effectiveness but need to improve communications and capture a full view of your customers across sales and services teams, then a CRM solution could be just the ticket. Similarly, if you're looking to replace those Excel-based sales forecasts with a standard, automated system, CRM is the way to go. But if your customers have told you that you need to dramatically improve the value your sales team delivers, you need more than a software tool; you need to transform.

3. *Would a one-time event, such as a team meeting or leadership off-site, help solve the challenge?* While motivational speeches,

team-building exercises, and seminars may be helpful motiva-tors, they are not transformational. These events could be use-ful and informative components of a transformation—great for morale and incremental gains. But sales forces facing sweeping market changes, mergers, and other dynamic changes won't likely transform who they are and how they sell based on any one-time event. There is no silver bullet. Transformation has lots of mov-ing parts and interdependencies. This degree of complexity often derails transformation initiatives, and in many cases, this is the reason why executives never even try. Every situation is unique, and you must take time to understand the mechanics. Then, let the facts drive you, not the other way around. That's why in chap-ter 5 we'll walk you through an as-is analysis—a no-nonsense, no-holds-barred method of determining where your organization is—the knowledge of which is a prerequisite for transforming it into something new.

4. *What is the gap between your ideal state and what you've got now?* Draw it out, write it down, or brainstorm it with your colleagues. How big is the gap between what you have and what you want? If it's big enough, you may need to transform rather than tweak. For example, if getting there involves the whole organization (HR, IT, marketing, product, operations, etc.) not just sales, you're prob-ably talking about transformation. Are you aiming for relatively small incremental increases in sales? That may require change (such as training, new technology, or a motivational workshop), but not transformation. If you were selling a product and now you're selling a solution, getting your sales force to make that kind of change may require a transformation. After all, we're not talking about selling more widgets more efficiently, but chang-ing the way the sales force sells, the way sales are measured, and the way the rest of the organization supports sales. Does closing the gap simply involve more effort on the part of the sales team? Or does it require a whole new approach to sales? The former suggests a tweak. The latter suggests transformation. If the sales team must change its entire focus to be more customer-centric

as opposed to product-centric, then that paradigm shift suggests more a transformation than a tweak. We'll offer you a detailed assessment framework in chapter 5.

A sales transformation is not a journey for the fainthearted. There are a number of reasons for that, from the potential for sales leader and team turnover to people's overall resistance to change to the pressures of bringing in revenues while implementing changes to the challenge of building new skills and capabilities. Transformation requires staying power, consistency, and commitment from sales and executive leadership. Yet, with an average tenure of 18 months (according to an annual survey from CSO Insights) who can blame sales leaders for seeking "quick fixes" that might show incremental improvement this quarter while neglecting structural challenges that require significant time and effort to change?

Answering those four questions will begin to help you understand whether your sales force needs to transform or change. Again, each of those tactics may be necessary for your sales force. Each can support transformation, but they are neither structural nor are they transformative on their own.

## *Moving the Immovable Force*

In our experience, successful sales force transformations are the result of a top-down, systematic approach. It starts with the development of an overarching sales model to continuously assess and improve seven key elements common to every sales transformation, and it moves along a continuum illustrated in figure 1.1. In chapters 4, 5, and others, we'll focus on setting a vision and applying proven change leadership techniques to a transformation initiative step by step through what we call the Way of Sales. The Way of Sales addresses the "what," "why," "who," and "how" of understanding what's driving your transformation, implementing it, and—most important—sustaining it.

As we'll detail in the coming chapters, we've found that when we work with organizations to deconstruct each of these elements, analyze

**Figure 1.1** The Seven Steps to Sales Force Transformation.

them, and reconstruct them in alignment with the company's goals, our clients see significant, measurable, transformative results. True and lasting transformation requires hard work—harder than reading a book or signing up for a workshop. But when done properly, the results of transformation are well worth the effort.

How do you get a sales organization to rise above the transformation dilemma and make profound and sustained changes? Let us examine a few areas at the outset: leadership, the human factor, and the desire to change.

### *Leadership*

In any team setting, especially with high-performing teams, individuals look to their leader as well as their peers for support. In sales, this is especially true with top performers. We celebrate their success on posted leaderboards, bring them on stage at sales and president's club meetings, and structure incentive compensation plans that lavish rewards on these high achievers. But what happens when a top performer doesn't support the need to change? Perhaps this individual is successful due to isolated factors that are not scalable across the team (e.g., a unique sales territory or customer relationship). We often see top performers who are already implicitly operating with many of the desired future-state behaviors and skills but are reticent to embrace new processes or tools, if only to demonstrate to other team members, who look up to them, that they are on board. What do you do with top performers who revolt either openly or in passive-aggressive ways? Sometimes you just have to cut your losses.

Jim Dougherty, a senior lecturer at MIT's Sloan School of Management, recalls an anecdote from his days as a sales leader. "In two cases we had to have summary executions," he told us. "We had a very active guy who was saying that the [transformation work] we were doing was crazy. Our head of sales met him at the Atlanta airport, fired him on the spot, and took his computer and his phone. Within an hour, everyone in the company knew about it. And we saw more productivity right away."

Another executive we interviewed, the senior vice president (SVP) of global field operations for a $3 billion high-technology firm, shared a similar story of making an example of those who are either unable or unwilling to change. He announced a major transformation initiative. "We wanted everyone who wanted to be part of the change to be successful." He told us that he communicated this message to his sales team, "If you have the willingness to change, you can. But if you don't take advantage of the opportunity, you'll be gone." The company had launched a sales force transformation after 10 straight quarters of flat or declining revenues. This firm had excellent technology and respected engineers, but it was being outsold in the marketplace (confirmed through win/loss and voice-of-the-customer research). The company sought to transform its sales force into a solutions-focused team with vertical expertise and end-to-end solutions that included hardware, software, and services. As part of the transformation, the company hired new vertical sales specialists, expanded the software and services teams, and deployed a new sales process that outlined how and when the core account managers should engage the specialists.

During the initial deployment, there were two perennial top performers who were vocally opposed to the need for specialists. The SVP met with each of them to understand their concerns and reaffirm the case for change and his expectations. Three months after the first wave of changes, these two account managers hadn't changed their ways, so the SVP dismissed them. This took guts. Given the financial performance and the fact that this transformation was "make or break," it took a strong backbone to make these changes. But 12 months later, the company had grown sales by 17 percent.

## *The Human Factor*

Before we go any further, let's not forget the issue of human behavior around transformations (and even around some tweaks). As many as 99 percent of sales transformations are driven from the top down. In many cases a new leader or someone looking to spark change initiates the transformation. But the fact is, the further you get from the boardrooms, the less the need for change will resonate. Success will depend upon getting everyone at every level of the organization engaged.

Human behavior is hard to shape. Salespeople must be able to connect to the need for change. If there are no direct, visible benefits (monetary, territory, new clients, opportunity for advancement, overall growth, client retention, etc.), don't be surprised if your sales team seems less than thrilled when you try to implement a transformation. People do what they need to in order to get by and sustain the levels of success required for their personal situations. Everything sales reps hear from "corporate" is filtered through some degree of skepticism. So when you want to make a change, you're up against opinion like the following:

- "Here we go again, another new executive with a big idea."
- "I'm just going to keep my head down and stay out of the way."
- "Why are we doing this?"
- "Who thinks this is needed?"
- "Did we ask our clients if they want this?"
- "This will only last as long as the new executive does."

Your role as sales leader, both in tweaks and transformations, is to address these questions systematically and reverse the possible negative human behavior that may be emerging. The sales leaders' job is to let the team members know that what is good for the company is in fact good for them. But the only way to demonstrate this commitment to your team is to be present. Go run some sales calls (we know, novel idea), ask team members for ideas, create champions, uncover what motivates them now, and take the first step to being *visible*. Too often we uncover very early that the executives seeking transformation have *not* been in the field at all or only with very strategic customers. And now they want a major change? This drives sales reps' skepticism—and often their resistance.

For example, a large print media company with 1,000 sales reps was looking to "rightsize" the business. The organization was made up of franchises, which made change even more complex because the sales reps at the local franchises felt that what corporate wanted was all well and good, but corporate didn't sign their paychecks. The transformation was aimed at becoming a more financially responsible company, improving margins, and making the shift to a comprehensive media (print and digital) offering. The company had to change the conversation it had had with advertisers, and this was hard. Where did the transformation initiative die? For one thing, financial responsibility isn't relevant to the franchises unless it lowers their costs or drives better margins for them. And this wasn't visible at the franchise level. A well-rounded media offering sounds great, but the sales reps made *zero* dollars on digital ad sales—so why would they invest their time and resources in selling digital? And as for changing the fabric of each conversation with advertisers—the reps found that almost impossible, and since no executives actually got out and sat in on any sales calls, the reps realized that the management had no idea what they did on a day-to-day basis. And what human behavior showed up among the reps?

- They called one another to complain about the stupidity of these ideas. "Ignore them and they'll go away," they said of the corporate pests. (Meanwhile, there was an immediate loss of productivity.)
- There was less employee engagement overall. In this case rightsizing triggered résumé buffing.
- Loss of confidence that corporate can successfully steer the business.
- Loss of key executives who knew the change was misdirected.
- No change at all to the sales presentations being made in the field despite huge spending on "customer messaging" from corporate.

Human behavior is a powerful and logical force in tweaks and transformations. As we peel the onion more, we will study success and analyze some mistakes in order to help you get this right. This is a tough hill to climb, and expert guidance can save time and enhance success.

### Desire for Change? Rarely There!

At the beginning of this chapter we described "Jane's" efforts to launch a global sales transformation focused on the goal of becoming a "world-class" company and her assumption that all her salespeople would go along with the transformation because they wanted to be world class. In our interview with Jane about 20 months after she launched the sales force transformation, she reflected on the main challenges: "The number one challenge is getting the sales teams' heads around change, the need and desire for it," she told us. "The desire for change is rarely there. Early on when I sat in the corporate office, I believed it was obvious that when things weren't going well, we had to change. But it wasn't obvious to all. You had to paint the picture with enough of a ramp-up time so that the need for change was compelling and felt real to them."

In the next chapter, we'll cover the levers of sales transformation—the methods and tools required to analyze your current conditions, make leaders aware of the need for transformation, align the initiative with the organization's strategy, measure results, and communicate about the work.

### Chapter 1: The Transformation Dilemma—Takeaways

- Change in a sales organization is different—and more challenging—than in other functional areas.
- Qualify your sales force for transformation as the marketing department qualifies a lead: by asking the right questions.

- Differentiate between a tweak and a transformation; what does your team or organization require?
- To move the immovable force, you must focus on your top performers and influencers in the team or organization.
- Organizations that neglect to address the human factor (skepticism, resistance, avoidance) often risk seeing their transformation efforts fail.

# CHAPTER 2

# The Levers of Sales Transformation

"**W**hich levers do I pull to improve sales performance?" We hear that question a lot from sales executives. Just as a CEO is interested in revenue growth, operating margin, incremental investment, and other factors that impact the company's stock price, sales executives want to ensure they are leveraging the right things to increase the success resulting from their sales transformation.

The concept of a lever with respect to sales force transformations came from a conversation with David Mears. David worked for 18 years as an executive vice president with the BayGroup, where he led sales force transformations with numerous clients. David told us about the challenge of leading the change: "Everyone will take a shot at everything you're trying to do. You'd better stand up to friends and foes, have the power to say no or yes, and have the power to support what you do. If we pull the key levers...and focus on the key forward-looking indicators, you will be on the path to a successful and sustainable change."

Before we describe the six levers of sales force transformation, let's take a brief look at what, exactly, a lever is.

## *Amplifying Change*

The word "lever" comes from the French *lever*, "to raise." A lever amplifies, or raises, the force you put into it, and in this way it puts out an even greater force. The ratio of the output force to the input force is known as the lever's ideal mechanical advantage. When you invest money, or time, or effort, you are seeking a similar ideal advantage. You want to gain leverage. You seek a maximum return on your investment. It's the same with sales force transformation. In almost every change initiative, resources are limited, and the transformation is expected to occur within a certain budget and time frame. And perhaps most important, at the same time the sales organization must continue to bring in revenues that fund the business. One of the big challenges is how to get the most return from your investment in change.

So, when considering a major change or transformation of your sales organization, what levers can you pull for an "ideal transformational advantage?"

We've identified six levers (see figure 2.1) that not only help to amplify and sustain change within a sales organization but that can be applied to almost any organizational change. They are particularly valuable with sales teams, however, because, as we outlined in the previous chapter, sales professionals can be highly resistant to change. In every successful transformation we know of, the leaders pulled most (if not all) of these key levers. How might they apply to your organization and which ones should be bolstered and reinforced?

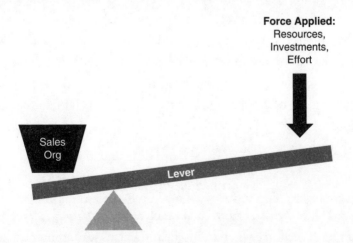

**Figure 2.1**  Sales Force Transformation Levers.

## *Lever #1: Perspective*

As we highlighted in chapter 1, much has been written about how the customer's buying process has changed over the past decade, mainly as a result of the Internet. In their book, *How Google Works,* Eric Schmidt and Jonathan Rosenberg succinctly describe three technological drivers of this change:

> Three powerful technology trends have converged to fundamentally shift the playing field in most industries. First, the Internet is made information free, copious, and ubiquitous—practically everything is online. Second, mobile devices and networks have made global reach and continuous connectivity widely available. And third, cloud computing has put practically infinite computing power and storage and a host of sophisticated tools and applications at everyone's disposal, on an inexpensive, pay-as-you-go basis. Today, access to these technologies is still unavailable to much of the world's population, but it won't be long before that situation changes and the next 5 billion people come online.[1]

We know the world is now better informed, but little has been written about what these better informed buyers want from their suppliers, vendors, or partners. Sales teams need a perspective to understand *why* change is happening. An outside-in perspective provides leverage because you are listening to the needs of those who will buy more from you if you get it right. An outside-in perspective is one in which the company elicits feedback and listens to what their current and prospective customers want, need, and value, and then develops or modifies its offerings accordingly. A number of companies we've worked with were so internally focused that they had trouble adapting to changes in their markets.

For example, one high technology client focused more on its margin-poor hardware portfolio even though the firm's customers found the margin-rich software to have more differentiated value. The client was traditionally a hardware provider in the telecommunications space, which was becoming more and more commoditized. Through an outside-in analysis, the company's executives realized that they could provide more value by focusing on software and simplifying their internal processes, such as quoting and billing, in order to make them easier to do business with. The company leaders gathered outside-in feedback through surveys of customers. They called these voice of the customer (VOC) surveys so that when disseminated throughout the organization everyone understood that their valued customers were providing this much needed insight. Other ways to gather VOC input include qualitative interviews, focus groups, and advisory boards. VOC data provide a critical view of the way outsiders perceive your organization by illuminating gaps and showing you where changes need to be made. For example, when we talk with customers of companies that have made numerous acquisitions, we frequently hear that there are many salespeople serving the same customer. One of our client's customers commented to us during a VOC interview that the client's "sales reps often meet in his offices," with each trying to sell his or her particular product line. It's important to leverage this outside-in perspective to help identify and prioritize gaps and frustrations from the customer's perspective. Some issues, such as overlapping sales coverage, may be easily identifiable while others are hidden or confusing (mixed messages about the value of solutions or the customer problems addressed, for example). In a nutshell, an outside-in perspective helps you look honestly at customers' perceptions, gauge the gap between the perceptions they have and the perceptions you want them to have, and then determine the way forward to close the perceptual gaps. What better way to accelerate a transformation than by completing an outside-in analysis? Why guess at the way your customers and prospects see you when you can find out by asking them?

The second part of gaining a perspective involves an inside-out internal review. What's working? What's not working? And how do you know? Do you have access to reliable and valid metrics? At the very least, the internal view should include an assessment of your strategy, people, process, tools, leadership, and metrics. The customer's or prospect's outside view must be balanced by what's possible on the inside. That's why your initial assessment should cover both perspectives: outside-in and inside-out.

Involving your customers and your sales team in the design of a solution is a great approach to leading change, and it is essential if you want to get this done successfully. We've worked with numerous clients who have created both external customer boards and internal sales advisory boards. The key to success with both boards is to select members who are seen as influential by their peers and have credibility in their areas of expertise. We remember one client who selected a seller who was considered sort of a pain in the sales organization as he seemed to question everything, but he was a real asset on the internal advisory board because he forced the sales executives to make the transformation messages clear and crisp. Like your customers, the members of your sales team know the problems they encounter. Leverage your discovery efforts to engage the stakeholders—your customers and key members of your sales team—who will make the sales transformation successful.

The results of these assessments will provide insights into the gaps between your status quo and your vision of the future, insights needed for your transformation roadmap.

Action steps:

- Review what it would take to start a customer advisory board even if it's only an informal one. At the very least, set up a conference call with key customers at least quarterly and ask a series of open-ended questions to get them talking about their experiences with your company and your competitors.
- Look at creating a sales advisory board made up of internal opinion leaders from sales and sales-related functions who will serve to validate assumptions and strategies, include people who tend to be direct, candid, and insightful
- Review the voice of the customer strategy and how the company is capturing input from both customers and prospects on an ongoing basis.

### Lever #2: Alignment

Everett Hill, SVP for Customer Development at Sipi Metals, remembers when he was charged with transforming a 1,200-person on-premises sales team for Coca-Cola Enterprises, Coke's largest bottler at the time. The primary goal of the transformation was to standardize and simplify the organization's sales approach that had grown unwieldy over time and had too many metrics and too many goals. As he set out to simplify the process, Everett quickly realized that no sales transformation would happen unless distribution made changes as well. In our interview with Everett, he told us, "One of the things we learned from the national data is you can't be successful selling if you can't keep the promises you made to customers. This spawned the distribution transformation project." This was exactly the same situation at Central Garden & Pet. In order to be successful from a customer's perspective, the sales teams needed to be able to deliver on their promises, and this required alignment with other business functions, such as distribution and supply chain. In Central's case, we saw a classic alignment gap: the sales team could sell certain products, but the supply chain couldn't keep up, resulting in stockouts, long delivery times, and unhappy customers.

These examples represent a key theme from our interviews and our own experience: Sales can't be an island when it comes to successful transformation. If the sales organization tries to go it alone, the transformation is unlikely to be successful, and by the same token, the organization cannot transform unless the sales team is a willing partner. A key lesson came from one of our interviewees, a sales executive of a Fortune 100 company on its third sales transformation; in hindsight he realized that he should have included other functions and stakeholders in his first two transformation efforts, neither of which had been successful. According to the executive, in a rush to get the transformation efforts started, the sales organization didn't create alignment or build alliances with other related functions. This organizational alignment concern was also mentioned in almost every interview we conducted: the most successful transformations involved approximately four sales-related functions up-front in the process. Think about a crew team in an eight-person scull: They all must be exactly aligned in order to get the boat going in the right direction—straight toward the finish line. The alignment required for success on the river is the same that's required to be successful in front of the customer. As counterintuitive as it may seem, complex B2B sales is a lot like competitive rowing: both are team sports.

Gaining alignment early on in your sales transformation provides significant leverage to your sales transformation, because your sales team (and customers) can immediately benefit from the support and resources offered during the transition, and specific requirements can be integrated (rather than waiting to see what sticks). Common examples include updating recruiting profiles and compensation with the support of HR, linking the sales pipeline and forecast to the manufacturing and product planning schedule, and updating messages and sales kits from marketing.

Action steps:

- Identify the key internal barriers and enablers to your sales transformation based on the gaps that need to be closed and areas that can be leveraged.
- Engage internal leaders from marketing, HR, IT, and other relevant departments in discussions about the vision for the future of sales and what's needed from their organizations to support the vision.
- Outline investments from profit and loss statements that are beyond sales and include them in the overall business case for your sales transformation, even if the investments need to be phased in over time.

### Lever #3: Leadership

Strong and engaged leadership is essential for any change initiative. In almost all of our interviews for this book, the importance of leadership came up. In short, most said that if the key leaders weren't committed to the change and helping to drive it, it was not going to happen. Ultimately, the vision and commitment must be top-down, and they must go far beyond new coffee cups or trite slogans.

Obstacles will appear. Everyone needs to stay focused on the endgame and the path to get there. "You cannot delegate," says Mike Woodard; having helped lead sales transformations at many Fortune 500 businesses, he pinpoints leadership as the single differentiable driver of success in sales transformations. The senior team must be "willing to sit at the table while the transformation is being discussed, planned, and executed," he told us during our interview. Sales teams, who are trained to pick up subtle clues from their customers, can immediately see when a leader is just giving lip service to an initiative. Sales leaders must set clear and realistic expectations through honest and authentic conversations with staff. All the stakeholders need to know the time lines and the costs of the transformation, but also what is expected of them in terms of messaging and support.

Leadership comes from several different levels, certainly the top, but also the first-line sales leaders, where sales initiatives often live or die. In one telling example, a former client of ours—a health care consulting firm with revenues of $250 million—wanted to change into a solution and outsourcing-oriented organization based on changes its executive team saw occurring in the health care industry. The company traditionally conducted time-and-materials projects in the health care market but found that the larger solution/outsourcing deals were more profitable and kept most of their resources consistently utilized. There was also less competition in the midmarket segment, and the executives felt they could effectively compete given their relationships in the industry and overall capabilities. Interestingly, the two sales directors in the United States (East and West) were split over whether to embrace a sales transformation initiative. The sales director for the western region led the change from the front, facilitating key meetings, tracking and reviewing key metrics, communicating about transformation constantly, and coaching his team in new solution-oriented behaviors. The sales director for the eastern division did not embrace transformation. He didn't track key metrics, didn't coach, and was barely present with his team. Later, some in the organization said he'd been on autopilot and didn't want to put in the work to transform. He also, admittedly, was not a "numbers guy" and didn't think that revenues and margins would grow that much by transforming. Ultimately, and not surprisingly, the western division grew its revenues by approximately 20 percent more than the eastern region. What's more, the leader who neglected transformation was eventually dismissed while the leader who embraced transformation was promoted.

Leadership and ongoing commitment provide the leverage to distinguish a sustainable transformation from a one-time training event. Beyond lip service, leaders at every level who can effectively model, coach, and reinforce the desired behaviors and practices provide the critical link between vision and implementation. By going beyond a one-time sales development effort, sustained and authentic leadership across all levels of the sales team provides a multiplier effect that helps to accelerate change.

Jim Dougherty, who has led sales transformations at Gartner, IntraLinks, and Prodigy, and is now a senior lecturer in Technological Innovation, Entrepreneurship, and Strategic Management at the MIT Sloan School of Management, echoed the need to have the support of leadership and the ability to drive changes and prove through actions that the transformation is not just another short-term fad. During our conversation with Jim, he told us the following:

> what you find at a company that you turn around, the bad people are fired early, the really good people leave early, and the people left are politically astute mediocre players. They are a cynical bunch. The biggest barrier we faced was the cynicism. If you don't have full support of either the CEO or board, you'll get people dragging their feet, digging their heels in, saying, "We've done this before, it didn't work then...." The reason we could do this at [our company] was I was put in by the board and had free rein. If I didn't have free rein, I wouldn't have been successful. But you have to take the pendulum as far back as it will go, and you find that the people who resisted change...they will get carve-outs that they'll use in the future to reverse your changes. So we said "these are the rules and everyone will stick to the rules."

Action steps:

- Ensure that your senior sales and business leaders are fully committed to the vision and case for change; if they are not, do not embark on a sales transformation.
- Conduct several leadership meetings and working sessions to give your first-level and second-level sales leaders the opportunity to react to, shape, and buy into the vision for the future and the roadmap for change.
- Have leaders document how they are leading from the front by describing what behaviors and activities—such as coaching, metrics review, review meetings—they are executing on an ongoing basis; this document should be part of their performance review.
- Create a sales leadership board to capture and share best practices among sales leaders.
- Before you launch your sales force transformation, review how each leader is evaluated and consider a 360-degree view and process so each is getting constructive feedback from their reports both during the transformation process and afterward.

### Lever #4: Sequence

According to Jim Collins's classic bestseller, *Good to Great,*[2] to become a great company not only must you get the right people on the bus, but you also have to get them in the right seats: "First Who, Then What." Perhaps counterintuitively, many of our interviewees echoed this theme, but in the opposite sequence. In order to recruit, select, and hire the right people, you first need to know what they will be doing—what knowledge, skills, and abilities will be needed to support a new sales process or way of selling with your customers. If the transformation involves moving to a solutions selling model or to a split focus between existing and new accounts, these sales strategies require different skill sets and, often, different people.

For example, we worked with a Fortune 50 company that had a lot of great products, but little direction and no roadmap. Most of the company's profits came from a commoditized product, and leaders had no plan for focusing customers on their strategic offerings, such as servers, IT services, and software. The strategic offerings had significant competition from best-of-breed providers and other large technology companies. The majority of the business units lost money, and not surprisingly, a lot of their best people left those same units. In addition to a clear overall integrated business strategy, the marketing and sales organization was missing the "what" of enablement and strategy, for instance, providing integrated solutions to their customers' enterprise business and technology challenges. Part of the enabling underpinnings of a sales transformation is a clear, cogent, and compelling strategy, which can be more challenging for a large, global, multibillion dollar company to communicate and execute than for a smaller firm. This client solicited feedback on lever 1 (perspective) both internally and externally, and based on customer input developed a vertical, industry-focused solution strategy that better aligned enabling technology with the unique requirements of banks, hospitality companies, and consumer products businesses. Once that enabling story and sales strategy were in place, this company was able to attract the "who" and then get down to the "how." In this case, the company needed sales and sales support resources with deep industry knowledge to complement the IT/technology acumen the sales teams already had. Though counterintuitive, it's often true that high performers want to be in an environment that has some structure and direction. They find that they are most creative when working within that paradigm. For example, we have found that many sales professionals would rather work within a defined buyer-aligned sales process than in some chaotic system that is not documented or defined. The "what" of sales should be documented, defined, and actionable in order to attract the right "who."

Jim Dougherty also provided great examples and insights from his experience:

> In each and every case, the most consequential change we made was finding who the ideal customer is and why. At Passport Health we found there was a specific customer subset that matched with their proposition: It was hospitals with 200 beds. Once we determined that was the

sweet spot—the people below didn't buy for a whole bunch of reasons, people above didn't buy for a whole bunch of reasons, so that's how we approached it—marketing and sales, everyone focused on a big enough market segment. Six hundred hospitals that met that description and fifty were our customers. That meant 550 were open, around the customer profile. We did the same thing at Gartner, we determined who to sell to and who not to sell to—and why. That was a key piece. It helped us organize. Then we'd say, "What's the best profile of a sales rep to sell this? How do we compensate them?" Learning who to sell to is as important as learning who not to sell to.

The key lever here is somewhat counterintuitive, but by focusing first on what changes are required to implement your vision, you can reduce churn in your sales team by creating a sharp focus on the skills and talent required to implement your future sales strategy.

Action steps:

- Ensure that the "what" of your sales strategy (processes, governance, etc.) is defined and documented before you decide "who" to put in the roles and "how" to manage the team.
- Map out the skills, knowledge, and capabilities needed by your sales teams; if product or industry knowledge is required, make sure your sales force gets it.
- Update your success and recruiting profiles accordingly and then use these to assess your current talent and future needs.

### Lever #5: Measurement

The vision and the metrics you use to quantify the sales transformation should focus on the vital few things that will determine success or failure. In our survey we found that the number one predictor of success was whether or not a company measured progress. But keep in mind, it's a big world filled with data, and you can't measure everything. In fact, if you try, you'll end up measuring nothing. One client we worked with was measuring 180 KPIs, but no one really knew where the business was headed. The client ended up doing a balanced scorecard approach and went down to seven key metrics to track. These metrics were intimately linked to the heart of their sales transformation effort — things like revenue growth greater than run rate growth, wallet share, and contract renewals. Metrics we've found to be key in sales transformations are shown in table 2.1.

Ultimately, if you don't measure anything, you can't transform. We've seen too many organizations that produce metrics based on whatever data people can easily get their hands on. This results in too much data, redundant data, and irrelevant data. Thus, select a few vital metrics, such as sales growth or wallet share by customer, win ratios, or voluntary turnover, especially metrics that link directly to your goal and vision.

One former client of ours used pipeline data in addition to win ratios and sales-cycle velocity metrics to help transform the sales organization. The $2 billion data and services provider wanted to have a data-driven sales process and better understand what was moving in

**Table 2.1**   Key Metrics in Sales Transformation

| Metric/KPI | Description |
| --- | --- |
| Wallet Share | The share or percentage of addressable spend you have with the customer. |
| Win Ratio | Percentage of pipeline that the sales team is winning over some specified time period. |
| Gross Margin Growth | Generally, it is calculated as the selling price of a product less the cost of goods sold. |
| Average Deal Size | The amount of all deals that are won divided by the number of deals won. A good indicator of whether the team is selling solutions rather than single products. |
| Voluntary Turnover | The number of salespeople leaving voluntarily as opposed to being prompted by the company. |
| Sales or Revenue Growth | Yearly, quarterly, or monthly growth in top-line sales or recognized revenue. |
| Up/Cross-Sell Rates | The amount of add-on sales of additional products or services to existing accounts. |
| Participation Rate | The number of sales professionals who are achieving their goals/targets/quotas. |

and out of the pipeline on a monthly and quarterly basis. The sales leaders hypothesized that slipped deals (where close dates keep moving out) were not closing at even close to the rate of those that had some urgency and were won within a quarter. Through research and analysis, the sales leaders determined that they were winning just 15 percent of slipped deals, but 55 percent of in-quarter deals. The client reevaluated why deals were slipping and what attributes might signal whether that would happen. The sellers became more attuned to buying signals and the needs of their customers. Overall, by focusing on a few key sales metrics, the sales leaders helped to amplify a set of sales behaviors they wanted more of: conducting in-depth needs analyses, gaining access to decision makers, and better differentiating their offerings from the competition.

If you can't measure growth in bottom line or top line at the outset of your transformation initiative, what progress, outcomes, or growth *can* you measure? If you want the transformation to take hold, you'll need to show the C-suite compelling metrics and data. This process typically requires a high-level business case that demonstrates how leading sales effectiveness metrics (such as average deal size, length of sales cycle, or win rate) can be positively impacted by your sales transformation to boost sales productivity and overall revenue growth.

Metrics are a lever as they are a proxy for what is important to the company and sales organization, and they focus leadership on what measureable targets they need to reach and exceed. Almost all clients we've worked with have been interested in benchmarks and target setting so they can measure themselves against others and against a goal or target. Business in general, and board room discussions in particular, are heavily focused on metrics, often financial ones, but also very much ones related to sales—revenue, margins, return on investment or assets, inventory turns, and free cash flow, among others. Lastly, as important as new metrics are, the ones that you get rid of are just as important (to forget and stop tracking). What you stop is as important as what you keep.

Action steps:

- Identify three to five key metrics that you want to impact with your sales transformation and identify current metrics that have no impact.
- Determine if there are checklists being utilized to ensure that progress is being made from a process standpoint.
- Ensure that there is a component of a quarterly or annual review that looks at behaviors you want to reinforce or change (quantitative metrics and qualitative drivers)
- Ensure that each sales objective has a metric that includes a target (plan) and the ability to track actual.
- Identify an example (perhaps from a pilot or existing team) that you can measure and leverage to prove that the changes to the sales team will work.

### *Lever #6: Communication*

The greatest vision (or offering for that matter) in the world is useless if no one knows about it. We've worked with a number of clients where the sales organization created some great new processes and sales aids, but because only a few people knew about them, those innovations "died" from disuse. In one case, a client created a robust buyer-aligned sales process that was launched at a global sales kickoff meeting at the MGM Grand in Las Vegas. We've all been there: semi-dark room, everyone's tired, or otherwise impaired from the festivities that went late into the night before, and the SVP of global sales takes the stage. In an incredibly well produced event, the SVP brought in several customers via a live video chat, including CIOs from global Fortune 500 organizations, to describe the value they received from this company and how much of that value was shaped by the interaction with the sales team. Based on this type of customer feedback, the company was rolling out a new customer engagement process and supporting tools and training. It was a wonderful event and launch, but three months later, there was no visible communication or training regarding the changes, and there was no reinforcement through coaching and inspection from the first-line sales leaders. The sales leadership team was later reshuffled, and the process never got a chance to become institutionalized. When a new sales executive came in and found out about the process, he couldn't believe it was not being used and soon became its new communication champion.

Many senior executives are surprised at how often they need to repeat themselves to demonstrate that they are serious about making a change. Aside from having to be early and often, communications should also be authentic and transparent for optimal results and resonance. As a VP of strategic accounts eloquently told us, "It's more successful when we are more transparent with the sales team about what we need to do. We put it in business terms for them by saying, 'we're getting fewer resources; we are going to do it this way.' They see what's driving things. The more transparent we've been with what's happening and what's driving it, the greater their understanding."

In terms of sharing the vision and program, we also know that people have different learning styles and communication preferences. It's important to share the vision in different ways. Some people are persuaded more by stories and case studies than by hard numbers; others are the opposite. And bear in mind that in any organization with high turnover, key messages need to be repeated often so that the new people will hear and embrace them.

Communication may be the most essential piece of what leaders do in conveying their vision, commitment, and ongoing sponsorship regarding a transformation. The essence of sales and marketing is communicating your value and difference and compelling someone to act. As we've stated previously, a sales transformation should be thought of as an internal sales campaign. As in a winning sales campaign, the right communications, at the right time, to the right people is critical to winning a competitive, complex deal or effectively making the internal sale for a transformation.

Action steps:

- Build an overall communications plan and calendar that goes deeper than global and/or regional kickoff events; plan to schedule team meetings—weekly, monthly, etc.—six months to a year in advance.

- Schedule a potential town hall meeting for all employees, depending on the size of the organization.
- Reiterate the message and strategy in one-on-one conversations with employees.
- Ensure that performance appraisals and management include the key metrics and behaviors to drive the sales transformation.
- Review communication tools such as email newsletters to continue to disseminate the new strategy and transformative message.

Now that you have a sense of what is and is not sales force transformation and an understanding of which levers to pull at your organization in order to effect real, meaningful, and measurable change, next we'll discuss how to build the foundation and craft the vision for a transformation.

### Chapter 2: The Levers of Sales Transformation—Takeaways

- Sales executives want to ensure they are focusing on the right things that will increase the likelihood of success from their sales transformation.
- Levers work by raising or amplifying the force that goes in, ensuring an even greater force comes out. That's known as an ideal mechanical advantage.
- To reach your "ideal transformational advantage" you need to pull the right levers in your sales force and across the entire organization.
- We have identified six key levers to pull for an ideal advantage in your sales force transformation: perspective, alignment, leadership, sequence, measurement, and communication.
- Successful sales force transformations nearly always involve pulling most if not all of these six levers.

# CHAPTER 3

# Building the Foundation and Vision of the Future

We were meeting with Mike Dickerson at his office in Atlanta early in the summer of 2012, and Mike had just taken on a leadership role for PGi's Global Collaboration Services. Mike was describing his vision for PGi: a transformation from a provider of dial-up conferencing services—which have increasingly become a commodity with an intense focus on price—to a software and solutions business focused on helping companies create more value through enhanced collaboration. Mike's and the executive team's vision was to implement this business transformation with new sales and go-to-market capabilities that would be tested with PGi's diamond accounts, their largest global customers. Mike described the need for a new way to engage with these customers; it would require more collaboration and consultation overall as well as function-specific insights on how collaboration can drive results. He also spoke of the internal capabilities needed to support this new level of customer engagement. These capabilities included a new account planning approach, standard sales and opportunity processes, and better resource alignment at an account level. Leveraging his background as both an entrepreneur and sales executive, Mike was able to describe his vision for what needed to change, why it needed to change, and why it needed to change now—all components of a solid vision for sales transformation.

As we described in chapter 2, the levers of sales transformation are critical to creating an ideal transformational advantage. But you also need to know what's driving your transformation and where you want to go. What is your vision for the future of the company overall as well as of your sales organization? Being able to describe the vision is crucial because that's how you will rally others and get them to buy into the sales force transformation. From executives to sales leaders, from salespeople to other internal organizations, from partners to customers, you need to sell your vision of a shining city on a hill. Otherwise, why would they go along? That's why, in every step of the process that we outline in the coming chapters, we'll remind you of the importance of the *vision*. It's your guiding light. It shows people where they're headed. As with any guiding light, you'll be lost without it.

### The Burning Platform

In our experience, most visions begin with a "burning platform"— an event that is so compelling that the status quo will simply no longer be possible. In 1992, organizational change guru Darryl Conner introduced the phrase "burning platform" into the world's business lexicon in his book entitled, *Managing at the Speed of Change*[1]. The metaphor came from a report Conner happened to be watching on TV about a catastrophic explosion that had occurred on an oil-drilling platform off the coast of Scotland. One hundred and sixty-six crewmembers and two rescuers lost their lives in what still ranks as the worst disaster in the history of North Sea oil extraction. Only sixty-three crewmembers survived the blast. Superintendent Andy Mochan was one of them. Later, from his hospital bed, he described having been awakened by the explosion and—badly injured—escaping from his quarters and making it to the edge of the platform. All around him was fire. Gazing down, he saw steel and other debris littering the water's surface. Because of the water temperature, he knew that he would survive no more 20 minutes if he weren't rescued. Despite all that, Andy jumped 15 stories from the burning platform into the water.

When asked why he took that potentially fatal leap, Mochan responded without hesitation: "It was either jump or fry." He felt he had no choice. The price of staying on the burning platform was too high. It meant certain death, whereas leaping would mean possible life.

It's easy to understand why business leaders may be reluctant to transform a sales force in the absence of a burning platform. If there had been even a chance that Mochan would have survived aboard the rig, he wouldn't have jumped. But there wasn't, so he did.

The drivers we're about to outline aren't as dramatic or as life threatening as what drove Andy Mochan to leap from the burning platform. But it's not hard to see the underlying point: In life, and in business, we are not inclined to leap into the unknown until the moment when the known poses too big a danger. And even then, some will respond by burrowing their heads even deeper in the sand, hoping against hope that the impending disaster will go away on its own. In this chapter, we'll cover how to alert and prepare the crew for a transformation *before* a burning platform forces everyone to take a fateful leap.

Vision makes the idea of future change compelling. In many cases, such as with Paul Duval at Central Garden & Pet, we've seen executives develop their vision for sales transformation and then leverage the drivers to frame up a business case. The business case is used to gain the commitment and resources from senior executives necessary to launch and implement the sales force transformation. At Central, both the CEO and the chairman of the board approved Paul's vision and the business case he made.

Beginning here, and continuing through chapters 4 and 5, we'll dive into our seven-step process of sales force transformation. As shown in figure 3.1, these steps include the following:

- *Drivers:* The forces, events, and circumstances that can compel the need for a sales transformation.
- *Vision:* A definition of the desired future tailored to the unique needs and specific goals of the organization.

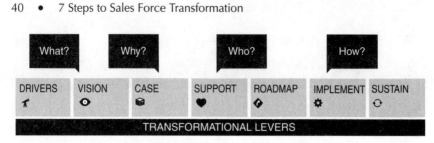

**Figure 3.1** The Seven Steps to Sales Force Transformation.

- *Case:* A description of what's required to build a case for change, which we summarize as an approach to treat your sales transformation like an internal sale.
- *Support:* Sales transformations require enabling support from other functional areas within the organization, such as marketing, HR, finance, and operations, as well as the external support from partners and customers
- *Roadmap:* A multistep process involving the formulation of strategy and structure, processes and tools, enablement and people, and metrics and management—all keys to a successful transformation initiative.
- *Implement:* How to launch your initiative, whether to roll it out as a comprehensive program or as a pilot, depending on factors such as budget, time, the size of your organization, and the degree of executive buy-in.
- *Sustain:* How to make the change "stick" through leadership, sales team training, communications, management tools, hiring, new hire onboarding, and beyond. After all, you can't expect the results to sustain themselves.

It all begins with the drivers that compel the vision for sales force transformation.

### Step 1: Finding Your Motivation (Drivers)

The drivers of a transformation vary across companies and industries, but at the highest level, they fall into a number of defined categories. In our sales transformation survey, we asked over a hundred sales leaders

**Figure 3.2**   What Drives Sales Transformation Initiatives?

and professionals, "What was the main impetus for the company's sales transformation effort?" As shown in figure 3.2, nearly half (46 percent) cited new revenue growth targets, and almost a quarter (24 percent) listed poor sales performance. New leadership came in third at 18 percent. The drivers might not necessarily be mutually exclusive, and they often overlap, but overall the results make sense to us. Transformations are not usually about desperate survival measures, but about unprecedented growth. They're not about avoiding bankruptcy, but about seizing opportunities. Some are driven by outside forces, and others by internal factors. But behind every successful transformation are one or more key drivers that served as a powerful motivation to change. Transformation is, after all, hard work. And let's not kid ourselves: there's risk involved. Let's take a look at seven major drivers and see which ones apply to your organization and which ones can serve as a case for change.

### New Revenue Growth Targets

We've seen a number of sales transformations launched as a result of flat or declining revenues. In our survey, almost half of respondents told us that new revenue growth targets spurred their transformation. This can be because the sales team is underperforming on revenue (sales), margin (operating or net profit), or both. One of the nice things about sales is that there's an easily identifiable scorecard: sales and margins. There might be many qualitative and behavioral factors driving sales performance, but the end results can be clearly measured. "Did you hit your number or quota?" is one of the most common questions of sales leaders and sellers.

Negative or flat revenue growth is often, a symptom of a bigger problem. It's usually noticed in the boardroom and on earnings calls (for public companies), but the problem is generally due to market or competitor changes or to the overall demand picture for the company's offerings. New revenue targets usually signal that a company can't just maintain the status quo. Growing the top line from 1 to 10 percent may require a transformation, which could be in the form of a new go-to-market strategy, new offerings, and different talents and skills. New revenue growth may mean a whole new approach to sales—and a transformation to make it happen.

Our research confirms our own experience: Many of the companies we've worked with began a sales force transformation because revenue wasn't growing fast enough. One client, a provider of technology to financial services companies, wasn't growing as fast as its competition; that was the major impetus for transforming the sales organization. The CEO was compensated based on growing faster than the competition, and the main focus was driving organic revenue growth (the company had historically grown through acquisitions and was pressured by Wall Street to prove the value of an integrated business model). The company was selling stand-alone products and not a full solution. Sellers often competed with their own colleagues in front of customers!

This company's sales vision for the future required the sales capability to achieve new revenue targets by offering integrated solutions that increased the value delivered to the customer while also growing the average size of deals for the company.

### Poor Sales Performance

In our research, missed sales/revenue targets were both a direct driver and an indirect one, influencing both new targets and new leadership drivers as described above. Causes and effects are not always easy to untangle or determine, and many sales transformations are launched to achieve improved financial results of some sort. Not surprisingly, a sales organization that consistently misses goals requires a change. The question is: how much of a change? Some companies that we profiled and have worked with directly required only incremental changes to improve performance while others needed to transform. Determining the difference is critical. Are you changing the oil or are you replacing the engine and transmission?

For example, one technology company we worked with had a global sales team of 150 employees and had experienced flat revenues for three successive quarters. Management wanted more attention paid to the company's top 50 accounts along with better messaging linking its services to several industry-wide trends: changing data regulations in the health care and financial services markets and the move to cloud computing services. With relatively straightforward changes, this company was able to grow revenues by 16 percent over the next two quarters and position itself to be acquired at a premium. Poor performance drove the need for changes within the sales organization, but there was no need for a holistic transformation.

Although poor sales performance may be a factor that drives transformation, it's seldom the only factor; in many cases, such as the one mentioned above, it drives *change* but does not require a full-scale transformation initiative.

## New Leadership

Another obvious transformation driver is new leadership. In fact, 18 percent of our survey respondents cited a new leader as the primary driver for transformation. New leaders often have different perspectives and philosophies about a business, an industry, or management styles. There are a lot of books in the marketplace on this topic (one of our favorites is *The First 90 Days* by Michael D. Watkins[2]). Many new leaders want to establish themselves by creating and driving some key transformational initiatives. It's been said that one of the best times for a seller to try to land a new account is when there is a change in leadership at the buying organization. New leaders, as opposed to those with tenure, are often more open to new ideas and to change. A change in leadership also signals that the status quo isn't working. It can be the first step to a more holistic sales transformation.

A new leader can serve as a powerful change agent, bringing in fresh ideas and outside perspectives. At a large consumer packaged goods (CPG) firm we know, a new CEO and SVP of sales were brought in specifically to transform the business after several years of declining results. These leaders were able to bring to bear best practices and lessons learned from their prior experiences and to use their positions to challenge assumptions about the status quo; they launched a multiyear sales and business transformation. The turn-around CEO (or head of sales) is often the one to "inject" change into the organization and turn it into a new direction, but there is usually only a short window of time to demonstrate improved results.

## Mergers and Acquisitions Activity

No surprise here. When two companies come together, the results can be awesome or they can be awful, especially when cultures, systems, and training don't match. In our survey, while only three percent of respondents told us that mergers and acquisitions directly drove their transformation efforts, many more were driven by the lasting effects of prior acquisitions. They might not have used the word "trans-formation." Instead, they may have framed it as, "We need to integrate two business units or companies. What do we do with the sales teams? Should we integrate the teams? Can one salesperson sell the full breadth of products and services? How should we integrate the teams?" Integrating teams from different backgrounds, different cultures, and different strategies requires more than basic change. It takes a transformation.

We have often seen a delayed effect from mergers and acquisitions. In some cases the acquired company acts in a stand-alone fashion while the overall company adopts more of a "holding company" or portfolio model, which leaves stand-alone sales and marketing teams. The driver for sales transformation kicks in when the organization decides to shift from a holding company model to an operating company with an integrated sales and marketing organization. In the case of private equity companies this often occurs when the investors start to plan for an exit. For example, one of our clients had acquired numerous companies and products and had a major issue when meeting with prospects and customers. There might be eight to ten sellers in the room, each vying to sell his or her product instead of an integrated solution based on the customer's needs and requirements. Customers were confused and frustrated, and this often lengthened the sales cycle, given all the coordination involved. Our client eventually streamlined the model so only three or so sellers would be in a customer meeting at the same time. This solution wasn't perfect, but it was an improvement (supported by improved win/loss rates and voice of the customer feedback). The three sellers would work with the other units in the background and not in front of the customer, thus providing a more integrated and seamless experience for the customer.

## Outdated Sales Methods and Teams

Organizations that emphasize traditional features and benefits selling should be careful. The Internet is arguably the greatest product knowledge equalizer in history. In this day and age, there's a good chance that your prospect will know about your product's features and benefits before you arrive for a sales call. If you rely on old-school sales techniques—and especially if you're losing market share—you may need to transform your sales organization by orienting the team to a new way of selling, and you may need to reexamine your core value propositions.

Technology has changed the dynamic between buyers and sellers. As documented in *The Challenger Sale* and other recent articles on the changing nature of successful business-to-business sales, the ability to leverage new methods of selling has become a key driver in keeping up with the competition and customers. Research by McKinsey & Company has found that early adopters of a "digital-enabled sales model are achieving two-times revenue growth rates, three-times customer growth rates, and 30 percent higher acquisition efficiency than businesses using the traditional sales model."[3]

Depending on what your company sells (for example, solutions, consultative services, business-to-business, business-to-consumer), your sales organization might not be able to keep up with how your customers want to buy. If that's so, your team may need to acquire new skills in order to be successful and meet customers' expectations. As we discussed earlier in chapter 1, training is not transformation per se, but it may be necessary for a transformation to take hold.

So how do outdated sales methods or teams drive sales transformation? If your organization has a significant cohort of salespeople who've been in the trenches for many years and who will likely retire around the same time, you may want to think about transformation as you prepare to orient a new group of salespeople. If you are in this situation, it may be time to transform your sales force into one that knows how to tailor your value proposition, provide compelling insights, surface unrecognized needs, and develop long-term business relationships built on measurable value.

### Customer Changes

In a world where technology is changing rapidly it stands to reason that customers' needs, tastes, and choices may change just as fast. When they do, their suppliers need to adapt. When the changes are small in scope, they might not affect the sellers who serve these customers. But when buyers change significantly, the change may impact all parts of the sellers' organization. Says PGi's Mike Dickerson, "In our case, the market changed. How customers bought information technology services changed. We found ourselves in the world of

Software as a Service (SaaS)." When PGi looked at what it wanted to transform to, it realized that companies were buying information technology services differently than before. And PGi's leaders thought about what that meant. "If buying and the use were different, then the way we approached generating revenues was different," recalls Mike. "Sales aren't about winning the new customer. No, it's about growing revenues. In the SaaS space it was about getting into an account and then driving adoption, not just going after the next logo."

At Coca-Cola, an external factor—national obesity awareness—drove the sales organization's transformation initiative. "[Consumers] were moving away from carbonated soft drinks to carbonated water, water, and fruit juices," says Everett Hill, who, as we mentioned earlier, led sales transformations for Coca-Cola Enterprises. "Coke dove deep into four hundred thousand accounts and then made a key decision to more aggressively market fruit drinks and water products." For a while, the company didn't want to think about a worldwide trend away from carbonated soft drinks toward healthier choices, but eventually there was no way to deny the trend. The new portfolio presented new opportunities, but as Everett points out, "it also required a new way to sell" by a transformed sales organization that had to think beyond carbonated soft drinks. As is often the case, this transformation was driven by an external factor—in this case, changing health trends—that led to an internal driver, new product lines.

This driver in particular reminds us that transformation is not a one-off, but a continuing journey. As a former IBM sales executive told us, "If you're in sales transformation, it's every day. You're always in sales transformation. The reason you're in it is because the person who dictates that you're doing it is the customer. The customer decided one day they're not going to buy from you, they're buying from the competitor. So you say 'Oh jeez, what are we doing? Too pricey? Too remote?'" When you know the answers, then you go about making the changes required either to get that customer to come back to you or at least to stanch the hemorrhaging. This is an ongoing process of assessing your customers, learning to anticipate market changes, and adapting to customers' demands.

## Product Changes

In our conversation with Steve Young, formerly of AT&T, MCI, and Verizon and currently on the faculty of Georgia State University, he talked about how changes, launches, and sunsetting products can drive a sales force transformation. The core products his organization was selling, outbound voice and data, were experiencing negative growth. Looking for growth elsewhere, the company came up with seven or eight new, strategic products (including network security, call center outsourcing, managed services, data centers, and managing those data centers) in a number of vertical industries it hadn't previously serviced. In order to be successful and make up for the slow revenues in the core areas, the sales force had to learn how to sell a new portfolio of products in industries the company had not sold to before. Because hiring and training a new sales organization wasn't feasible, Steve knew he needed to transform the sales force he had, and that's what drove his initiative. Moreover, in conjunction with the previously mentioned transformation driver, customer changes, product changes often result from a change in what customers value, but they can also shape the market in terms of what customers didn't know they wanted (think Apple). Given the challenge of trying to be a product innovator, many companies develop products so new that they require a transformation of their sales organizations.

### Step 2: Creating Your Sales Transformation Vision

Now that you've established that there are one or more compelling drivers for change, you need to begin thinking about what level of change is required; this is step 2 in the overall transformation process. Is your vision big and bold or is it more focused on incremental change that can realistically be achieved in about three years? Is your platform actually burning? If your feet are hot enough, it shouldn't be hard to make a compelling case for transformation. After all, it's jump or die.

In the coming chapters we'll discuss how to assess your current state, determine what level of change is warranted, and develop a sales transformation roadmap. But for now, keep in mind that like any major project, your sales force transformation must start with a powerful vision and then follow a defined plan or roadmap to make it real. That's how businesses get started, technology develops, novels get written, and skyscrapers get built. Moving from a vision to reality—with a lot of hard work in between—is mostly common sense. But as the French writer Voltaire reminds us, "Common sense is very rare."[4] In the heat of a quarterly sales battle, in the midst of trying desperately to make your numbers, in the middle of a slow year, when you're in survival mode, common sense often flies out the window, along with the vision and any hope of lasting, meaningful change.

The bottom line on what drives a sales organization transformation: Not sluggish sales, but a burning platform; a compelling vision; a robust, adaptable communication strategy, top-down buy-in, a defined roadmap and implementation plan, and the will to stick it out, day after day. We'll spend the remainder of this book walking you through each of these essential components.

## How to Define Your Sales Transformation Vision

A lot of ink has been spilled on how to create company vision and mission statements. We have them too. A vision for a sales transformation should be linked to the overall vision for the company, but it is usually more specific to the sales organization. The classic quote, "If you don't know where you are going, any road will get you there" is relevant when it comes to setting a vision. A vision, quite simply, is a picture of what success will be at some point in the future. A great vision should be inspiring. It gets everyone in the organization excited and motivated to come to work. Qualitatively, a compelling vision can help a company to prioritize efforts, attract and retain talent, and accelerate time to value. In general, the more clearly you can articulate your sales transformation vision and high-level goals from the start, the less time and effort you will spend on trying to fix miscommunications, misalignment, and employee disengagement later.

We have had the opportunity to work with the American Red Cross's Biomedical Services division, which collects and processes more than 50 percent of the blood donated by volunteers in the United States. This might not be the first organization that comes to mind when you think about transforming a sales team, but the BioMed division has a large team that focuses on signing up churches, community centers, schools, businesses, and other groups for blood drives. The organization had experienced significant change due to competition in the blood donation market, changing regulations and technologies for blood collection and distribution, and significant changes in leadership (three CEOs in less than five years). The leader of the BioMed division had served as the interim CEO and was experienced in transforming other businesses in the biomedical field. He leveraged this experience and his firsthand knowledge of Red Cross's BioMed operations to craft an overall vision for change based on climbing a mountain. While this metaphor may seem like a cliché, this leader had was able to articulate a powerful vision of the specific areas that needed to change, the specific roles that other leaders needed to serve, and the impact on both customers and donors. He also demonstrated a key component of communicating a vision: storytelling. He was able to communicate his vision to everyone from his immediate management team to the volunteers staffing a blood drive at the local YMCA. His vision set the stage for a multiyear transformation at the BioMedical division that is still continuing today.

As with many business issues, setting and crafting your sales transformation vision involves answering some challenging questions. It will require deep thought and critical thinking. In our experience, a great vision for sales transformation requires addressing a few fundamental questions regarding your customers, your value proposition, and your ways of communicating this value to your customers. As you answer the following sales-specific questions, you will begin the process of writing and rewriting your vision:

- Customer Segmentation: Who are our customers/segments?
  - What is the profile of our ideal customer?
  - What is the value we provide (or should provide) to our customers?
- The Selling Conversation: What's the value proposition? What do sales conversations with these customers and stakeholders sound like?
  - Has the customer's buying process changed? What value do customers expect from our sales team(s)?
  - How important is the sales process and team in communicating and providing this value to our customers?
  - What new or different sales capabilities are required to continue to drive value for our customers?
- Business/Go-to-Market Model: Do we have the optimal revenue and cost structure to support the desired business and go-to-market model?
  - How much revenue do we need the sales organization to bring in?
  - What is the targeted cost of sales?
  - At a high level, have we outlined the go-to-market model to execute on our sales transformation vision?

As you answer these questions, keep in mind that there is a vision for the company as a whole, which is often broad and far-reaching, but there also needs to be a specific vision for the sales force transformation, a vision that can guide the teams regarding which customers to target, what sales conversations to have, and how to integrate themselves into the go-to-market model. Let's explore each of these three areas in detail next.

## Customer Segmentation

One of the most fundamental questions in business and sales is which customer segments to pursue. There are numerous models for selecting the best segments. Some of the key attributes include whether the segment is measureable, whether it's substantial enough to target, and whether it's accessible. From a vision standpoint, you may be targeting the wrong segments, or you may want to double down on certain segments given the market opportunity and your ability to differentiate your business from the competition.

For example, a hospitality firm that operates midscale hotels and targets blue-collar or grey-collar customers is unlikely to gain much traction selling to the software, financial services, or pharmaceutical industries, which mostly use upscale hotels. There's no product fit. When crafting a strong sales transformation vision, you need to articulate not only what segments are a good fit for the company, but also how those segments might change in the future. What's the profile of the ideal customer now and in the future? We've seen numerous visions that include a much greater focus on the largest accounts (for example, more resources, coverage, touches) while optimizing the cost of sales in pursuing small and midmarket customers using an indirect channel and/or an inside sales team. In short, your sales transformation vision should include some guidelines for identifying the ideal segments and customers so that your sales teams pursue the right accounts and opportunities.

## The Sales Conversation

As a part of formulating your sales transformation vision, you need to determine the type(s) of customer conversations that are required to effectively communicate the value of your products and services. The complexity of the customer problems and needs that you address dictates different selling models, many of which may already be in place, and these may vary for different customer segments as illustrated in figure 3.3, adapted from Neil Rackham's insightful book, *Rethinking the Sales Force.*[5]

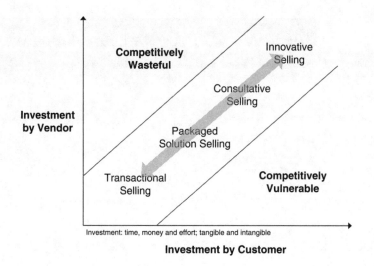

**Figure 3.3**  Selling Models.

A key point is that innovative selling is not necessarily *better* selling. While both innovative and consultative selling on average deliver greater value from the standpoint of a sales team and its capability, this type of sale is more expensive and has a longer sales cycle. Besides, not all customers or situations need these types of solutions. For example, consider how the process of buying a car has changed in the past 20 years. Thanks to the Internet, information sources such as Kelley Blue Book and automobile manufacture's websites, which contain sophisticated configurators where you can build your own car, consumers can navigate the purchase process without the assistance of another human being. Tesla has certainly capitalized on this change with elements of its direct sales model. What started 50 years ago as a consultative sale has now fully evolved to a transactional one, putting the automotive sales force at risk unless it changes.

Innovative products often, but not always, require a unique and sometimes one-to-one selling capability (think of the iPhone in 2007). The best model is one that matches an appropriate level of investment with the corresponding and desired value to be provided to the customer. A sales transformation vision should profile the ideal customer; it should describe the value the ideal customer expects, and it should articulate how the company will serve that customer.

| | Transactional | Solution (Packaged) | Consultative | Innovative |
|---|---|---|---|---|
| **Client Expectations** | Accessible; Easy to procure | Easily understood; Ready to deploy | Problem solving; Joint solutioning | Shared risk/ reward; Unique offerings |
| **Value Definition** | Low cost; Undifferentiated | Easy to implement; Time-to-value | High ROI and competitive advantage | Unique benefits; Market creation |
| **Target Role** | Procurement | Business Unit Leaders | VP/SVP/EVP | CXO Level |
| **Optimal Channel** | eCommerce | Indirect channel; Direct: Territory rep. | Direct: Account executive/mgr. | Direct: General or Business Mgr. type seller |
| **Sales Cycle** | Minutes | Weeks | Months | Months/Years |
| **Relationship** | Light | Light to Moderate | Deep | Deep and Interdependent |

**Figure 3.4**   Selling Models Defined.

A few more details on the selling models shown in figure 3.3 follow below (summarized in figure 3.4):

- *Innovative* selling is characterized by collaborating with your customers to develop new or unique solutions. Some common examples include strategy consulting, investment banking, and enterprise technology, where the customer collaborates with the supplier on the design and specifications for a custom system. This selling model requires a high cost of sales and investment in deeply skilled and experienced resources for interacting with customers as well as for support before and after the sale. The model may also include substantial executive-to-executive selling as the companies may jointly go-to-market with a cocreated offering. A hallmark of an innovative sale is providing unique value that ultimately serves to differentiate both the customer and the supplier. In our experience, innovative sales represent less than 5 percent of the selling teams and capabilities out there today.

- *Consultative* selling is characterized by providing advice that transcends the value of the product, service, or solution. This type of model exists in many industries (including enterprise software, professional services, and emerging technologies). Neil Rackham has said that a hallmark of consultative selling is that after the sales meeting, the customer is so impressed with the value of the discussion that he or she is willing to write a check for your time alone, whether or not he or she purchases your product or services. A true solution, in our definition, may have predefined components, but these are configured in a way that's specific to a client's situation. In our experience working with sales organizations in many industries, we have found that the consultative sales model represents less than 10 percent of the selling teams and capabilities out there today.
- *Packaged solution* selling is characterized by sales teams/organizations differentiating themselves both on what they're selling (the package, bundle, or product) and on how they sell and serve the customer. In our definition, a packaged solution doesn't require much customization or tailoring to be ready for the client. The goal of the seller is to sell the product, package, or bundle as is. We've found that this type of solution selling represents anywhere from 30 to 40 percent of sales today and a vast majority of the business-to-business sales conversations. Many of these conversations are not consultative and can still resemble glorified product or catalog reviews.
- *Transactional* selling is characterized by sales that are of a commodity nature, both in the product and in how they are bought. Examples of this type of selling can be found in professional services (staff augmentation), retail banking (personal loans, credit cards, etc.), or many maintenance, repair and operations (MRO) services. Transactional selling models represent at least 50 percent (and much more in some industries) of the sales transactions today, an amount that is growing.

Note that your business and customers may require several sales models based on the customers' needs, buying process, and the targeted cost of sales; we'll cover this next in the go-to-market model.

## Business or Go-to-Market Model

Once you understand which customer segments you want to pursue and the types of sales conversations you want your teams to have, then you need to ensure your go-to-market (GTM) model is aligned with those objectives. GTM questions might include the following:

- What channels or routes to market make the most sense in reaching our selected segments?
- Should our sales conversations occur through a direct (employee) field seller or through a partner or channel?
- How do our customers want to interact with us, through what channel and means?

The most effective GTM model is one that is closely aligned to the product portfolio and the routes to market. For example, you aren't going to sell a multiphase, complex system integration project via the web or the phone. It also doesn't make sense to sell commodity paper clips via an expensive direct field resource. As you craft your sales transformation vision, it's important to articulate how your GTM model will change to better align your offerings, channels, segments, and conversations.

Congratulations! You now have the core components for a sales transformation vision. But keep in mind that a vision has no intrinsic value. Like a map, it's a useful tool, but without the hard work to make your vision a reality, it won't get you anywhere. What you have before you is a starting point, one that you'll refer to repeatedly throughout your sales transformation. As indicated in the story at the beginning of this chapter, Mike Dickerson had to talk about his vision at least a hundred times to drive Global Collaboration Services forward. He constantly referred to his vision as his Rosetta stone for making sure his teams were headed in the right direction. The vision is a necessary but not sufficient condition for a sales transformation. For example, you can have a vision for how physically fit you want to be at the end of the year, but you have to do a lot of exercise over many days, weeks, and months to achieve your goal. It's no different for a sales transformation.

---

### Sales Transformation Vision Checklist

- **Customer Segmentation:** Who are (and who are not) our customers?
- **Customer Conversation:** How do we adapt the sales capability (and investment) based on the target customers and their expectations of value?
- **Solutions and Value Propositions:** Can marketing/ product management enable our sales team(s) with customer-specific value propositions and customer-ready messaging and collateral?
- **Expected Outcomes:** What value does our transformed sales capability bring to our customers, our company, and our investors?
- **Initial Business Case:** What is our initial estimate (order of magnitude) investment required to transform (which will be refined in the roadmap stage) the sales organization?

---

### After the Vision: Heavy Lifting

Your sales transformation vision should be your guiding light to which you'll look again and again to motivate and orient the sales organization. As Michael Conway told us: "You have to provide a vision of what the transformed organization would look like and how it would operate so that you can create the demand in the organization and so people want to transform. They have to see that the pain of transforming is worth it for the rewards that will await them at the other end, that there is a better way and that they can get there. You need to connect with people emotionally so that they want to be associated with the transformation and the resulting organization."

In keeping with our "no silver bullet, no magic pill" mantra, your vision will differ from that of another sales executive depending on the reason for the transformation. If you're transforming from a service provider to a solution provider, your vision will likely look different than it would if you were transforming after a merger of two different sales organizations with different cultures. If you're transforming because your biggest customer changed its business model and you now must reinvent your sales processes, your burning platform will probably look different from the one if you're transforming because of poor sales performance.

### Chapter 3: Building the Foundation and Vision of the Future—Takeaways

- Sales transformation is often driven by the urgent need to seize new opportunities for growth.
- The vision for sales transformation must include the burning platform for change, which is typically formed around one or more of the main drivers of successful transformations:
  - New revenue/growth targets
  - Poor sales performance
  - New leadership
  - Merger and acquisition activity
  - Outdated sales team skills
  - Customer changes
  - Product changes
- Your vision needs to clearly articulate your desired future for sales, internally as well as regarding the types of conversations to have with customers, and the value provided by the sales organization.

- Your vision will evolve based on how you segment your customers, the value your customers expect, the sales conversations you have with them, and your go-to-market model.
- Your transformation will roll out differently than others based on what your organization is transforming from, what it's transforming *to*, and what's driving the transformation.

# CHAPTER 4

# Treating Your Sales Transformation
# Like an Internal Sale

I n our research on sales force transformations for this book, the greatest challenge mentioned in both the interviews and the survey was achieving sustainable change in a sales team. Even though sales teams and leaders excel at convincing others to change, they are typically highly resistant to change themselves. It's no accident that there are five steps required to complete in our approach to sales force transformation before moving to implementation, and this chapter focuses on steps three and four: building your case for change and gaining internal support.

Our experience and research have taught us that you should handle a sales transformation effort just as you would a hard-fought, drawn-out sales campaign, but in this case, the campaign is focused internally on your organization. As in an external sales campaign, you need to have not only a sales strategy but also a relationship strategy for capturing the "votes" of the key stakeholders, whether they are the sales star we just described or key members of the executive team. As with any sale, you'll need a strong and compelling value proposition that is tailored to each group of stakeholders. Keep in mind that although some sellers are "coin operated," others, like that sales star, are motivated by rewards that aren't exclusively monetary.

What is the compelling need for change? You have to be able to describe it in terms to which your audience will relate, terms it will find engaging.

A sales transformation effort can be a significant budget item that "competes" with other initiatives and programs for funding. So your internal sale to the "financial buyers" may involve convincing the executive team to allocate resources and sponsor the effort. As in an external sale, the level of sponsorship will be based on the size of your organization and the "signing authority" of the executives. In the case of Central Garden & Pet, the CEO and ultimately the board of directors approved the investment in a sales transformation effort. At several Fortune 100 clients that we've worked with, the senior vice president of sales and division presidents provided the final approvals and funding. Based on your organization's size and structure and on the scope of the transformation project, you'll need to target the appropriate funders and sell to them like you'd sell to a financial buyer at an outside organization. In several cases, the initial business case for the transformation effort wasn't approved and required either a proof-of-concept pilot or a refined business case and persistence from the sales leader to ultimately prove the initiative's value and gain agreement.

### Steps 3 and 4: Building Your Case for Change and Internal Support

Let's look at how the key components of an effective sales strategy apply to your positioning as you "sell" a sales force transformation in your organization. We've identified the following six core components of common customer-facing sales strategies that should be applied internally in selling a sales transformation:

1. Clearly articulate the value proposition.
2. Develop executive and organizational sponsorship.
3. Equip sales managers to lead the change.
4. Gain buy-in from the sales team.

5. Show immediate value.
6. Leverage a program/project plan.

For each component, we've outlined the action steps you should take that incorporate some key change management principles.

### 1. Clearly Articulate the Value Proposition

In sales, it's fundamental that people make a decision to purchase only when the perceived value received equals or exceeds the costs. In many cases, the value transcends money and can be more personal in nature (recognition, for example, or promotion or job security or, as in our earlier example, free time). This same concept applies in sales transformations: sellers and sales managers need to see that the "pain" of transforming is worth it for the rewards that await them at the other end. It's also important that the chief sales officer (CSO) and sales leaders communicate the value proposition. In general, sellers have more respect for the direct line sales leaders than for a support function, such as sales operations or marketing communications, both of which should play a big part in helping to implement and enable the transformation.

The best examples that we've seen typically combine both internal (rewards for the sales team and company) and external (benefits for customers, partners, investors) perspectives. One of our clients in the industrial services market sought to increase the efficiency and productivity of its field sales team and branch operations resources. The operations team was mainly involved in qualifying and quoting new projects. From a salesperson's perspective, the branch operations staff members were "free" resources; in fact, they were anything but. Our client determined that the company's cost of sales was almost 25 percent higher than the industry average; most of this higher cost was attributed to the involvement of branch operations resources in poorly qualified opportunities. To change the behavior of the sales team members so they would utilize sales support teams more effectively, the company leaders made three changes:

1. They implemented an opportunity qualification scorecard to ensure that the right opportunities were being "invested" in.
2. They began tracking time spent by sales support resources on opportunities, such as branch operations time.
3. They added an overall team bonus based on productivity.

Sales reps began to see the value in better qualifying opportunities. They started to engage support resources once the deals were qualified, and this increased the overall win rate and reduced the overall cost of sales while giving the sales team an opportunity for a new productivity bonus. By linking the desired changes to key sales metrics and incentive compensation that the sales team could control, the company was able to improve its overall win rate by 23 percent while decreasing the cost of sales by 14 percent.

Just as with an external sale, the value proposition for your sales transformation (the internal sale) needs to engage your different customers (for example, the sales force) in ways that are meaningful to them and at points where they can impact the organization. We've seen a wide range of successful tactics and list some examples below:

- A large media company we worked with was rapidly losing clients due to eroding results and a limited advertising budget spread across a growing number of platforms. The sales reps had been resting on their laurels (existing clients) for too long. In order to get the sales reps' attention, management cut base salaries by 30 percent, and all new business was rewarded with the highest possible commission. Not surprisingly, this resulted in outrage and a few exits of sales reps. But this was a way to let the real "hunters" stand out. The reps received those high commissions on net new deals for the first full year of their customers' orders—ensuring that they sold the deals right, not just as "one-time" wins.

- A technology company with over 1,000 reps we worked with was heavily focused on improving collaboration and communications among internal sales teams in order to better serve hundreds of strategic accounts. The main issue was that numerous people from the company were calling on the same customers in an uncoordinated fashion, annoying customers and prospects and leaving opportunities on the table. A full-day session brought the different sales teams together and helped them combine and integrate their overall knowledge of each strategic account. After the session, all deals "tagged" as collaborative in the company's CRM system allowed for two or more sellers to get compensated as long as they worked together to craft the solution for the customer. The results? A more than 100 percent increase in the size of the overall sales pipeline and millions of dollars in monthly repeatable revenue. The payoff in terms of a higher cost of sales from a team selling model was now well worth it.

- Another information technology company leader had serious issues with sellers focusing on the one or two deals in the funnel that represented a chance to quickly meet their quota. If one of those deals slipped, got pushed or went away, the reps wouldn't have enough other active deals, resulting in missed goals and poor team performance. This company's sales force transformation involved getting the whole team engaged and focused on the team's mix of opportunities in terms of size (for example, $10K to $100K per month) and stage in the sales process. A new scoreboard was developed to show each rep's opportunities. The expectation was clear: you need deals at $10K, $30K, $50K, $75K, and $100K+. The reps received points for each opportunity in the ranges assigned, and prizes were awarded weekly as they filled the scoreboard like a game. (Think: "What's behind door #4 for an opportunity worth $75K?") The team members needed to win the important, large deals, but they also needed enough smaller opportunities in the sales funnel to still make their number if the big deals push out a quarter or two, which they often do.

The key attributes of most effective business-to-business sellers are that they are autonomous, self-motivated, entrepreneurial, proactive, and creative problem solvers. Those with some tenure have most likely been successful so far, so why should they change what has worked for them? The characteristics that make a successful seller are often the opposite of the ones that make a person easily absorb change from the corporate office; therefore, it's critical to "sell" them as you would a customer. As we've seen in these examples, it's essential to connect the value of your sales force transformation to what's important for an individual salesperson. We've found that the sales team's favorite radio station is WIIFM: What's In It For Me.

Action steps:

- *Create a Feedback Team*—Create a small advisory team of sellers and sales managers to test communications and value propositions with, and then refine and revise the program based on their feedback.
- *Define Value*—Understand how each internal target audience (for example, sellers, sales managers) defines and measures value, just as you would with a prospect. This understanding will be a key component of crafting a customized value proposition for each group.
- *Articulate the WIIFM*—Make sure you clearly articulate the "What's in it for me" (monetary or otherwise) and value for the sales team in your transformation plan and communications.

## 2. Develop Executive and Organizational Sponsorship

As our friend and former colleague, Tim Sullivan has told us, "Politics: you don't have to play the game, but you can't ignore that the game is being played." Sales teams often spend a significant amount of time trying to understand who has power and influence in a customer's organization as the decision-making process and authority at many organizations isn't accurately documented on an organizational chart. Like many sales professionals, we (the authors) have had several experiences where we have been tripped up in sales cycles because we didn't fully know, appreciate, or respect the informal power of someone with a relatively low official title or overestimated the power of someone with a lofty title. There are many books written about selling approaches focused on mapping the customer's organization and identifying the sources of both formal and informal power and influence. These are foundational skills in almost every selling model.

We have found that these misjudgments apply equally to sales transformations, especially so when a company is organized by regions or business units with leaders who are responsible for their own profit-and-loss performance. In these cases, an overall sales leader must often work through influence, as opposed to fiat, in order to drive changes in the sales team, especially one that is organized in a matrix structure. The sales leader must gain the support of the regional and/or business unit leaders along with the support of senior executives. We have found that the larger the organization, the more time you will need to invest in understanding the politics and formal/informal decision structure of the organization. As a former head of sales for several global companies told us, "In retrospect, I would have spent more time managing up."

We have worked with several Fortune 2000 technology companies that cater to financial services organizations. In each case, these companies had grown through acquisition and had strong business unit leaders and cultures. As these companies sought to transition to a more integrated selling model, they have established an overall sales leader who essentially serves as an "overlay" to the business-unit-led sales teams. These sales leaders have had to work through others to accomplish their goals (for example, increased customer "wallet share," improved customer satisfaction scores, lower cost of sales) and have leveraged small wins along with overall executive support to drive their sales transformations.

In addition to obtaining the support among executives and other sales leaders in the company, gaining the support of other functional areas is a critical success factor, as we discussed in chapter 2 in the "Levers of Sales Transformation." In our research, we found that leaders often involved other areas, but not always, and this was a key regret for many looking back (see figure 4.1).

Often, the leaders of these functional areas, such as human resources, information technology, and marketing, have mutually exclusive or even conflicting goals. We've seen several successful examples where leaders of a sales transformation have engaged these critical, cross-functional stakeholders; a few examples follow:

- Aligning goals and an individual bonus (often through management-by-objectives) of the functional leaders to the desired outcomes of the sales transformation. A leading US telecom firm linked each function's management-by-objective (MBO) portion of compensation to the specific goals of the sales transformation. For the sales leaders, they linked 20 percent of their variable pay to the "participation rate" of their teams, defined as the number of team members achieving their sales targets.

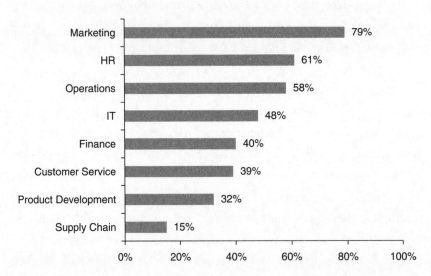

**Figure 4.1**   Gaining Organizational Buy-In.

- Creating a cross-functional transformation program team with representatives from each key functional area who have the ability to lead change and communicate the WIIFM to their respective function. In one example, a technology firm that sold to financial institutions had grown through the acquisition of several small and midsize companies. One of the key elements of the firm's successful sales transformation was to enlist the sales, marketing, and human resource leaders who had previously operated in an autonomous and entrepreneurial manner to communicate the case for change and lead the change in their respective organizations.

Just as you would map out the customer's organization in a major, complex sale, you must apply a similar approach and rigor to your own executives and peers as you seek their support and sponsorship for your sales transformation.

Action steps:

- *Determine the Power Structure*—Identify the key influencers and approvers ("voters") for your sales transformation across the organization and at multiple levels.
- *Build a Communications Plan for Key "Voters"*—What will resonate with each of them? For marketing leaders, the key point could be increasing the value and use of their "sales-ready" messaging or increasing conversion of marketing-generated leads. For human resources leaders, you might show how the sales transformation will reduce voluntary attrition. Map out the best methods and messages for engaging these individuals and their teams.

## 3. Equip Sales Managers to Lead the Change

Part of the strategy of many sales campaigns is to identify one or more sponsors who will sell on your behalf in their organizations. In some sales methodologies, a "coach" is someone who will provide you with internal guidance and feedback; a sponsor is not only a coach, but someone who will advocate for you when you're not in the room. Similarly in sales transformations, you need your own sponsors (or champions), but in a different level and role: first and second line sales managers who can provide constant and ongoing reinforcement and coaching to the sales team. As Lisa Redekop, the former global head of Sales Academy, Learning & Enablement at Thomson Reuters told us in an interview, "If you don't have hands-on support from your front-line managers, you can have the best salespeople in the world, but the change will not be sustained. A great sales manager knows how to motivate your sales talent and that it's not all about the top 1 percent. It's more about enabling the salespeople who are at the top 20 percent—if you can get more out of them you are getting more than if you motivate the top 1 percent."

First and second level sales managers must provide authentic leadership. They must be prepared (and equipped) to model, coach, and reinforce the desired behaviors. Sometimes this requires additional resources/support. After all, many sales leaders have never been taught how to coach. Steve Young, the former telecommunications executive we introduced you to in chapter 3, told us about a coaching program he implemented almost accidentally: "I had a sales manager from New Jersey out on maternity leave. She called me when she was going to come back. I said, 'You have a job, maybe not the same as before, let me talk to your branch director.' She said that she didn't want to be a sales manager anymore. She wanted to be a coach. I thought, 'Soccer coach? Basketball coach?' She had gotten herself certified as a coach, she told me. I started her off on that basis, and we ended up with eight coaches spread geographically across the organization. That is what got me started thinking about things other than 'beating up' on salespeople." This coaching program allowed Steve to better lead and drive changes within the sales organization. We cannot clone the perfect sales manager/leader so it's critical to invest in building the capabilities of this team in your sales organization, both to lead and sustain your transformation, as well as to provide the ongoing guidance, development, and supervision to your sales team.

Finally, another common element of sales campaigns and sales transformations is the sales management cadence: an ongoing measurement, inspection, and management of the sales process in the former and of the change program in the latter. A management cadence is nothing more than a schedule for weekly, monthly, and quarterly meetings (some one-on-one and some as a team) to discuss such topics as accounts, opportunities, sales calls, and overall performance. Those meetings can spawn coachable moments in which a sales leader can help to enable changes regarding the thinking and behavior of the team.

The most successful sales transformations—those that achieve their goals and sustain them—all have enlisted and enabled their frontline sales managers to champion the change. For one of our clients, the first initiative in a sales transformation effort was to deploy a sales management excellence program. The program helped align the sales managers on a new sales process and sales management cadence as well as show them how to coach their teams on a more consultative sale. The client wanted the sales managers to "lead from the front" and to be part of a new way of selling for the salespeople. At the end, over 200 sales managers across the globe were equipped to better manage the new sales process and to coach their teams in a way that supported the sales transformation—messages and metrics were consistent across geographies and teams. The client felt strongly—as did we—that the sales managers needed to be experts in the new way of selling first, before the sellers had to, in order to feel confident in modeling and reinforcing the changes.

Action steps:

- *Build Coaching Competencies*—Build in (up-front) coaching development and resources for your frontline sales leaders, even if this includes matching them with experienced coaches. This cannot be outsourced; your sales leaders must show that they are changing to adopt and adhere to the new way of sales.

- *Develop Sales Leader Materials*—Provide the sales leaders with simple tools to help them put the new way of sales into practice and integrate these materials into their key selling/coaching moments; these tools should cover areas such as pipeline reviews, pre-call coaching/meeting preparation, and deal reviews. Make it easy for your sales leaders to practice what they preach.
- *Celebrate Sales Leader Successes*—Look for and communicate/ celebrate sales leaders who are leading the way. A common lagging indicator is an increase in a sales leader's participation rate, that is, the percentage of team members who exceed their goals or quota. Early indicators include feedback from the team (180/360 degree feedback), increase in pipeline size and quality, and up-to-date and detailed account and territory plans.

## 4. Gain Buy-In from the Sales Team

In addition to the sales leaders, you must win over the hearts and minds of your top performers. Especially in sales, the sales team will look to the top performers and opinion leaders as models. If these key individuals are on board, the rest will follow. It's no different from an external sales campaign where you develop sponsors and identify the decision makers, the approvers, those who support you, and those who support your competitors. You need to connect with people emotionally so that they want to be associated with the transformation and the resulting new sales organization. And you must reinforce the messages and value proposition about the transformation—every day. Then focus on the process, and the results will come.

Fast Track Tools CEO Ken Revenaugh, a leader who not long ago transformed a company's sales organization, recommends that the vision you set should resonate with your salespeople's past experiences. "Build that burning platform for change," he told us, "and you get the early adopters and champions who say, 'This is like past experience. We should all do this.'" According to Ken—and we've seen this ourselves as well—usually someone will take you aside and tell you that what you're saying resonates with him or her. That person is a potential champion. A few years ago at a packaging company, Ken's group handpicked a few salespeople and sales leaders they thought were ready for change. Champions who are vocal and passionate are indispensable. In terms of buy-in, sellers and sales managers are often jaded, distrustful, and cynical. There may be significant "scar tissue" from previous change efforts in the sales organization. Imagine the classic sales kickoff that includes a big speech about how the upcoming year will be different and better thanks to the transformation gimmick du jour, such as a new way of selling, new technologies, new people, or some combination of these. There's nothing intrinsically wrong with a kickoff meeting; it's a way to communicate to all the sellers at one time, but without ongoing changes to processes, tools, and coaching, the message can quickly become hollow.

In a sales campaign, you are often seeking to maximize every interaction with the prospect or customer. One of our sales mentors was a senior partner at a global consulting firm and talked about finding opportunities to get to know prospects: "We had a relationship development program," he told us. "We'd find out what hotels they [prospects/customers] were staying at, and try to stay there; or where they were having coffee, and we'd just happen to be there. It's a diligent process." Internal sales transformations are no different in terms of the need to make every interaction count, and above all, consistency regarding the objectives and value proposition is critical.

One challenge with gaining buy-in from the sales team is that most sellers work out of regional offices or their homes. Change is much easier to drive when people are at the same location, when champions can spread the word at the water cooler, and when managers can more frequently coach and monitor in face-to-face contact. With salespeople, you have to optimize every second, and you have to minimize time out of the field. Even conference calls can become difficult as customers and geographical differences make timing and attendance a challenge.

We've found that sales teams do best with bite-sized pieces of change that they can absorb at one time rather than with a litany of items that become diluted and forgotten. Moreover, some times of the year are better than others for rolling out changes—the beginning of a quarter or a year, for example, or right after annual planning. You want to find times when you already have the sales teams' attention and then add small bites of change accordingly. Like a lot of marketing messages, change messages should be reiterated frequently and in different forms and should include stories, data, and personal engagement.

One of our clients structured an entire communications strategy based on the voice of the customer and the company's top performers. This software company interviewed more than twenty top-performing salespeople and frontline managers and shared these interviews through brief videos that were leveraged at sales kickoff meetings, regional town hall meetings, and an ongoing internal email campaign. The company had previewed the changes at an annual sales excellence club (an annual gathering of top performers) in Hawaii, enlisted salespeople's support and buy-in, and leveraged their voices to communicate the case for change and the value of the transformation to their peers.

Action steps:

- *Build a Stakeholder Map*—Just as you would map out the customer's organization in a sales campaign, identify your leaders and key influencers and get them on board immediately through directly communicating with them, involving them in the process, and asking them to play a leading role in the transformation.
- *Brand the Transformation Program*—Show and communicate to the team what is different about this effort compared to previous efforts (examples might include allocation of resources, coaching and inspection from sales leaders, or alignment of metrics and incentives.)
- *Connect to Your Vision*—Ensure that you and your team are able to leverage your drivers and burning platform to consistently make the case for change (and include the value proposition from step 1).

- *Define Talking Points*—Map out a series of events and also define core talking points for your leaders, including those influencers identified in step 3, so that everyone can stay on message, especially in informal interactions, which are often the most influential.
- *Anticipate Questions/Objections and Practice*—Just as you would before a significant prospect or customer presentation, practice your communications. Have your key stakeholders and leaders practice delivering the messages and role-play handling anticipated questions and objections.

## 5. Show Immediate Value

Given the overall need of the sales organization to show progress and wins, it's important to think about change this way. It's especially important in sales to have some quick wins and show progress toward the vision. Just as sellers need to show how they are growing their pipelines and advancing opportunities on a weekly basis, the sales leaders need to do the same with the transformation. They should mention the change on a weekly basis, and each month they should use a scorecard to show progress toward the vision (see figure 4.2 for an example). Rolling out a few quick wins can really engage the sales force. In addition, consider how you can pair a change that you are asking your salespeople to make with another change that takes work off their plate.

| Sales Center of Excellence | Key Account Management | O | Webinars & Communications | ◉ | Territory Sales | O |
| Customer Marketing | Cadence & Integration | O | Content Management | ◉ | **Key:** Issues – requires attention | O |
| Enabling Technologies | Sales Excellence Portal | O | Sales Force Automation | O | Mixed results | O |
| | | | | | Solid results/ progress | ◉ |

**Figure 4.2** Sales Transformation Scorecard.

For example: "If you can complete this win or opportunity plan template, you will no longer need to fill out this separate request for pricing approval, this other request for business development funds, and this third opportunity review form. We've designed the win or opportunity plan to encompass all of these elements and save you time." Show your salespeople how the change will make them more productive.

Michael Conway described how he put this into practice at Thomson Reuters: "We got some early wins and publicized them to show progress and keep the momentum alive." In the end, he says, the organization approached the transformation like a solution sale with a long cycle: "We brought into focus for sales a risk/opportunity that they were not keenly aware of, then helped them define what was possible and how we get there together. We started small with some proof-of-concept-type changes that were aligned to the overall transformation and earned our way into the follow-on sale of pursuing the bigger vision."

Showing immediate value is also important because sales teams often need to change "in-flight." They still have to hit their numbers; in fact, there is no other group that is as tied to the revenue engine as sales. They can't (and won't) devote hours out of the field or away from their customers to training, self-paced learning, or change workshops. One seller we worked with succinctly summed it up when he said, "I can keep selling the way I've been selling and make my number, or I can be the 'company guy' and focus on all of these change initiatives. At the end of the day, I'll keep my job if I make my number, and I'll lose it if I don't, so that is where I am going to focus." You have to find (or create) other ways to reach them. That can be a challenge similar to changing a tire while you're moving.

One of the best ways to balance the short-term need to show results and the long-term need for accuracy and effectiveness is to construct a pilot. A pilot provides the opportunity to test, show immediate results, and refine the sales model and components before a large rollout, and this can reduce your risk. However, a pilot requires time, so whether to create one really depends on the heat coming from your burning platform.

Action steps:

- *Identify Quick Wins*—Identify your best opportunities for wins (where the value will be received within a fiscal quarter) to build momentum within the organization and show early value to your executive stakeholders and approvers.
- *Celebrate Successes*—It's important to build success stories around the sales transformation that can be showcased and discussed. "Our team just sold a $1 million solution!" "One of our prospects said he liked the way we asked about his biggest challenge." Sellers can be rewarded and honored not just for their efforts but also for sharing success stories.
- *Quantify Value*—Executives and boards of directors pay attention to the sales division' numbers such as revenue, margins, and pipelines. As we've mentioned throughout this book, it's critical to ensure that the value from the sales transformation is measureable, quantifiable, and presentable in a format that leaders can easily consume, such as monthly/quarterly forecasts or other reports.

## 6. Leverage a Project/Program Plan

Many top performing sales professionals will leverage a project plan approach for a long, complex sale. Typically this plan will include major milestones and activities and responsibilities for both the internal selling team as well as the customer. It's a great way to ensure that as a seller, you're aligned with the customer's buying process and schedule, and you can track alignment throughout. For example, it's important to begin working through the legal terms and conditions for a contract well before the anticipated close date. If a customer balks at getting the legal team involved earlier in the sales process, that's a great time to ask some additional qualifying questions.

Similarly for sales transformations, program management and communications must be coordinated, ideally by a full-time internal resource; this is typically a senior sales effectiveness or operations leader who is well-respected in the sales organization. However, this should not be confused with the leadership role that senior sales executives must maintain early and consistently throughout the transformation and afterward to sustain the results.

Action steps:

- *Create a Program Plan*— Leverage an approach like the one outlined in chapter 5 to identify the major milestones and activities for your sales transformation.
- *Measure Progress*—Track progress and report to your sponsors and stakeholders on at least a monthly basis, with more in-depth reviews quarterly.

By now, we hope you see how critical it is to sell sales force transformation in-house—and to all your stakeholders—just as the sales organization sells your products or services. It's an effort that requires a blend of strategic and tactical actions. Now that you've got the organization behind you, you need to show everyone the way forward.

### Chapter 4: Treating Sales Transformation Like an External Sale—Takeaways

- Transforming the sales organization can create significant value, but it's often dependent on how you manage the change effort.
- Small changes in the sales organization can yield significant increases in value and opportunity throughout a company; they need not happen all at once to have a significant impact.
- Treat the sales transformation like a competitive sales opportunity in which you have to nail the value proposition, optimize communications, and gain stakeholder buy-in to be successful.

- Positioning your internal sales strategy involves the incorporation of the following key principles of change management:
  - Clearly articulate the value proposition—tune into WIIFM!
  - Equip sales managers to lead the change
  - Gain buy-in from the sales team
  - Optimize face time and communications
- Show immediate value where possible

# CHAPTER 5

# Building Your Sales Transformation Roadmap

The foundation of the sales transformation at Central Garden & Pet was the multiyear vision and roadmap that was created to prioritize and guide the overall effort. After our initial meeting with Paul Duval, the SVP of sales at Central Garden & Pet, we spent six weeks collaborating on a vision and a case for sales force transformation. This included ride-alongs with sales representatives and a plant tour in Madison, Georgia. There's no substitute for experiencing a day in the life of a salesperson and speaking directly with customers. In our up-front assessment we compared the current reality with Paul's vision of the future: a sales team with the ability to advise customers on how Central's products and services could impact the results of their stores (sales, gross margins, inventory turns). The current reality was characterized by a mix of skill sets, inconsistent processes, and limited use of technology. Through this assessment, we were able to identify and prioritize significant gaps and outline what needed to be done, for example, in the area of sales coverage, where there were several salespeople calling on the same stores, in sales planning where inconsistent strategies for the largest accounts were included, and in selling skills where more advanced skills were needed to create a more consultative sales team.

With an overall assessment, in-person interviews, and plenty of exposure to sales and customer conversations, we built a case for sales force transformation, and we charted an initial roadmap for Paul. This roadmap balanced the pace of change and investment with the sales team's ability to assimilate the changes: adoption of new processes, new sales skills, and in some cases, new customers. While we would all have liked to have flipped a switch to turn on an improved sales capability, it took time and several waves of changes, all guided by the sales transformation roadmap.

As we outlined in earlier chapters, a sales force transformation begins with an understanding of what's driving the need for change and a thorough description of your vision for a transformed organization. What does your desired future look like and how does it compare to your current reality? What are the gaps between these two situations? What will it take to close those gaps, and what's the value in doing so? The answers to these questions will help you establish a way forward.

This chapter covers step 5 in our sales transformation process; how to determine the required capabilities necessary to achieve your vision of the future and develop a roadmap to close the gaps between your current reality and that vision, a roadmap that's unique to your organization and situation. We covered how to develop your vision in chapter 3; in this chapter we will outline how to assess the current reality of your sales capabilities against our Way of Sales model to determine gaps. Once you've identified the gaps, you can prioritize these based on impact and ease of implementation to determine your major initiatives for your sales transformation roadmap.

Be advised, this chapter is like a workbook and will require some heavy lifting. Make no mistake about it: the gritty, unglamorous work of charting your organization and drafting a thorough roadmap is where many sales leaders and sales transformations fail. And it's where you can differentiate your organization and ultimate results from others that merely talk about transformation (and might be referring to training alone). Here's where you walk the talk. So let's roll up our sleeves and get ready to put real effort into planning your initiative. If your office walls are decorated with motivational posters, now might be a good time to take one down and replace it with something more actionable: the Sales Transformation Roadmap that we're helping you create.

## Gap Assessment

For many sales organizations and leaders, this assessment of the current reality requires a frank look in the mirror. It's like the Stockdale Paradox from Jim Collins's *Good to Great*. "You must never confuse faith that you will prevail in the end—which you can never afford to lose—with the discipline to confront the most brutal facts of your current reality, whatever they might be."[1] Therefore, once your vision has been defined, begin your assessment of your current reality—an as-is analysis of your organization. Don't assume you know what the problem is. Just look at the facts and make a realistic assessment. Don't guess. Observe. Measure. Ask. In our research, this up-front assessment is a critical success factor, but one that is often short-changed due to time pressures. Jim Dougherty emphasized this point in an interview when describing a sales transformation at a major technology research and advisory company. "By taking time to do the analysis you get to the end zone faster. It took us 11 weeks to figure all that out. The chairman was saying 'Why don't we have a plan? Why don't we have a plan?' It takes some patience to do that." Establishing as objective a baseline as possible is the most important thing to do, but there are diminishing returns. Don't get lost in an assessment loop where you are looking for a perfect baseline; plus or minus 5 percent or 10 percent will usually suffice.

The matrix shown in figure 5.1 is one way to depict the gap assessment between current ("As-Is") and future ("To-Be") states. We would assess each intersection point using some defined and standard criteria from the Way of Sales. At the bottom of the matrix, the underlying

| <Vision Statement> | | | | | | |
|---|---|---|---|---|---|---|
| **Way of Sales Areas** | **To-Be** | **As-Is** | **Gaps** | **Initiatives/ Programs** | **Execution Plan** | **Sustain Plan** |
| **Strategy & Structure** | | | | | | |
| **• S&S sub-areas** | | | | | | |
| **Processes & Tools** | | | | | | |
| **• P&T sub-areas** | | | | | | |
| **Enablement & People** | | | | | | |
| **• E&P sub-areas** | | | | | | |
| **Metrics & Management** | | | | | | |
| **• M&M sub-areas** | | | | | | |
| | **Perspective \| Alignment \| Leadership \| Sequence \| Measurement \| Comms** | | | | | |

**Figure 5.1**   Sample Gap Assessment and Program Plan.

levers from chapter 2 should be reviewed and can be analyzed on their own, as necessary. This is the matrix that will help to provide input for your sales transformation roadmap. For example, the roadmap may initially be sequenced to focus on quick-win gaps and areas that are "red."

For a quick walk-through of figure 5.1, you would first succinctly describe your vision, which you outlined as part of chapter 3. The vision should be your anchor and Rosetta stone for the transformation. Next, you'll think about your desired future for each Way of Sales area, which we'll describe more as part of this chapter. You don't have to be a ten (on a 1–10 scale, with 10 being the highest) in each area to be successful; some Way of Sales areas may be more important for your business than others. The next step is to do a rigorous assessment of your current situation for each area.

For example, are your market and sales strategies clear and compelling? Are your selling processes defined, actionable, and delivering results? Do you have the right sales talent and the development plans to grow the knowledge, skills, and abilities of the sales force? These and other questions will help you determine the current state of your sales organization: how much of a gap is there between where you are today and where you want to be? You also want to understand the nature of the gap. Is it a long-standing gap? Has performance stayed the same, but expectations have been raised? Has performance gone up, but expectations have gone up more?

Lastly, once the gaps are outlined and prioritized, you need to determine what initiatives and programs will help you close the gaps. This step is where you begin to generate the line items and rows for your sales transformation roadmap. These are the initiatives, programs, and projects that will be sequenced, unified, and managed as part of your transformation effort. The execution and sustain plans are also part of your roadmap, but they may also have additional, more specific elements.

Another benefit of your gap analysis is that you get to include your stakeholders in the development of the roadmap. As Jim told us, "Spend some time up front because the sales team understands the problems; they know what's going on. . . . I talked to employees and incorporated what they said into the plan, then went back to them and said, 'Here is the input you gave me, here is what will be incorporated, and here is what won't and why not.' Their fingerprints were all over the plan." We agree. Seeking the trust of the sales teams first and getting input from them is the single best way you can spend your time at this stage of your transformation effort.

### The Way of Sales

Defining a vision of the desired future state is a critical step in developing your roadmap. As discussed earlier, the sales transformation vision is more specific than the overall vision for the company. At the very least, it should include the customer segments you'd like to pursue, the sales conversations you want your sellers to have, and the go-to-market model you need to best reach and access your target audience. Each of those areas fits into our model for a Way of Sales, which is depicted in figure 5.2. Think of the Way of Sales as the key, or legend, to your transformation roadmap. Like topographic maps, a sales transformation

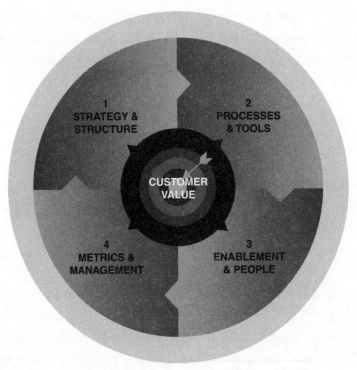

**Figure 5.2** Way of Sales.

roadmap contextualizes the elements of your sales organization to help you move from your current reality to your future vision. But on this map, instead of rivers and mountains, roads, parks, railroads, campgrounds, and other elements of the physical environment, you find the required capabilities necessary to achieve your vision of the future: all the key elements that need to be present, aligned, and optimized to have a high performing sales force.

Let's examine each of these four items in detail as they provide the framework for your gap analysis and your sales transformation roadmap.

## Way of Sales: Strategy and Structure

The classic quote from author and business strategy consultant Jeroen De Flander sums up why this area should be the first project on your roadmap, "You cannot be everything to everyone. If you decide to go north, you cannot go south at the same time."[2] It's hard to determine the necessary processes, tools, and metrics when you don't have an overarching go-to-market or sales strategy. The strategy is similar to the overall sales transformation vision; it's your guidepost for all the other Way of Sales elements.

A sales strategy clearly defines who you are selling to, what you are selling, how you are selling, and why you are different; it is based on the desired returns for the sales organization (revenues – cost of sales). In our interviews for this book, several executives told us that the first thing is to figure out to whom you should and should not be selling. That decision alone will inform everything else you do. It's a key piece in defining your sales transformation roadmap as the strategy informs everything that follows: the structure of the sales team(s), the capabilities, tools, people, and processes that are required for success. There is no one-size-fits-all strategy. For example, Amazon, which is best known as a business-to-consumer electronic commerce company with the world's largest online retail store, has also made significant forays into the business-to-business market. In the process of building the information technology infrastructure needed to support millions of customer transactions (in 2014, Amazon sold almost 5 billion items, or 159 items per second[3]), Amazon realized that it could offer its proprietary technology platform to other businesses (much as it opened its electronic sales platform to other businesses with Amazon marketplaces) and launched Amazon Web Services in 2006. When it launched, its target market consisted mainly of start-ups and web developers who sought to rent computing power and storage and would pay using a credit card via an online self-service interface much like the consumer retail site. Increasingly, Amazon Web Services has been competing with much larger and established technology companies, such as IBM, Hewlett-Packard, Microsoft, and dedicated cloud computing companies. Selling these cloud computing services to business customers reflected an expansion of Amazon's go-to-market strategy that required building an enterprise sales organization, and that is what Amazon did beginning in 2009. It's the same company, but with a different sales strategy and structure based on new customers supported by new solutions.

Most successful sales transformations begin as Amazon's did, with a question to determine the ideal customer. The answer will help to determine your sales strategy, structure, and roadmap.

The following strategic questions should also be considered in developing your roadmap:

- What are we selling?
- What is the customer (really) buying?
- What blend of new versus existing customers will meet our sales/ growth goals?
- How do we acquire new customers and grow existing ones?
- What can be spent on the sales organization to achieve the goals?
- How will the sales team be structured—by customer name or based geographic territories? Product or solution lines?

With the answers to these questions and the knowledge you gleaned from your assessment of your current reality, you can now begin to flesh out the enabling components of process, people, tools, metrics, and sales management that will form the key elements of your roadmap.

One client company we worked with, a technology hardware provider selling to large corporate customers, wanted to reexamine how it went to market—direct versus channel—as well as whether to focus on large, global accounts. In its current state, the client focused more on territories, but many of those territories had little market opportunity and distracted salespeople from what was actually driving the business: the top 5 percent of the account base. The structure needed to be more account-based, with the strategy for capturing higher wallet share and selling more differentiated solutions that included intellectual property, services, and hardware. Overall, once the client reformulated the structure and strategy, the company began to reevaluate its people and whether it could effectively execute the new strategy and the tools and processes to implement. The company's roadmap included workstreams focused on improving sales skills and hiring new talent, deploying new tools and technologies, and defining and adopting new business processes to support the strategy.

Your efforts to examine and roll out a new sales strategy and structure will take anywhere from six weeks to six months of behind-the-scenes analysis and modeling to produce a fact base that will allow you to design the appropriate go-to-market strategy and sales structure.

The maturity or readiness checklist shown in table 5.1 is a quick outline of the key areas to assess as you map out this step. It's not intended to be exhaustive, but to help start the conversation about some areas critical to your transformation's success. There's a checklist for each step. Make a note of how mature each implementation area is. Remember to talk with a few peers as well as members of the sales team to get a stronger sense of the organization's readiness in each area.

*Checklist Scenario:*

One of our clients gave his company a score of 1 or 2 on sales strategy and cost of sales. Based on some voice of the customer research, the company's customers wanted more of an end-to-end solution in terms of products and implementation services, which the company was not structured to deliver. As part of our assessment and recommendations, we refocused the company's strategy on three key pillars: (1) focus on the largest accounts, (2) rebalance direct/indirect resources, and (3) reallocate some of the support resources to improve overall cost of sales. The checklist helped our client to appreciate the need to review the company's account and territory design as well as its mix of solutions to improve the overall level of sales effectiveness.

**Table 5.1** Maturity or Readiness Checklist for Strategy and Structure

| # | Implementation Area | Rating (1–10) |
|---|---|---|
| 1 | Value and Competitive Differentiation | |
| 2 | Market & Customer Segmentation | |
| 3 | Account & Territory Coverage | |
| 4 | Balance of Direct/Indirect Channels | |
| 5 | Return on Cost of Sales | |

Rating: 1 = strategy for area is unclear/undefined; 10 = strategy for area is defined, documented, and robust.

## *Way of Sales: Processes and Tools*

A process is defined as: "a systematic series of actions directed to some end." Does this describe or even apply to sales? Mention the word "process" to salespeople, and you'll get a wide range of reactions from "management is acting like 'big brother' and inspecting everything we do" to a reluctant agreement that they follow, maybe unconsciously, a process themselves. In our experience, a sales process helps to define a predictable and repeatable path to sales success.

How your selling is done is greatly impacted by key processes, methods, and tools covering areas such as account and territory management, opportunity management, and your sales force automation (CRM) system. There are plenty of methodologies and tools available, including homegrown and hybrid approaches. The critical part of your processes and tools decisions is to implement the methods that best support and align with your sales strategy and structure, and the tools you choose should be leveraged and reinforced by sales leadership. As part of your assessment of your current reality, it's important to take inventory of what processes are defined, documented, and acted upon. In many companies, the process is basically an oral history that is interpreted differently depending on who you ask.

Jim Dougherty put a standard sales and pipeline management process in place at the high-tech firm where he spearheaded a sales force transformation. The changes he oversaw included a systematic approach to account planning along with systematic onboarding procedures. The goal, he told us, was to make the "planning process as efficient as you can, but obtain maximum value." When this was combined with an intense focus on the ideal customer (and who should not be a customer) as part of defining the sales strategy, the sales team grew their contract value for the first time in 14 quarters (since then, the company has sustained the momentum with 10 years of quarterly revenue gains). We have seen consistent results at companies from a variety of industries that have successfully implemented a sales process—and by "successfully" we mean in a sustained and measurable manner, beyond a training event or merely a tweak.

Starting with the ideal customer from your sales strategy, evaluate and note how your customers buy now and how they will buy in the future. What is their buying process? Where do they typically look for information? At what point do they consult with vendors or outside resources? Note, however, that even though most sales cycles are shown as a linear process, not all will follow this structure. When engaging in sales cycles involving consulting and insights (e.g., software, professional services), there may be more circular loops as relationships are cultivated and an intimacy with the client and key individuals at the client company is developed.

Key components of the sales process and tools area include the following:

- *Customer's Buying Process.* To define how your sales team should engage with your customers, you must first understand the nature of how they buy. What information sources do they consult? Websites? Analyst reports? Industry peers? Who's typically involved in a purchase decision? This should be an ongoing process because how customers buy is in a constant state of change as new applications hit the market. The buying process may also differ based on what the customer is buying (for example, using a request for proposal process for larger, more strategic purchases).

- *Customer-Aligned Sales Process.* This process helps to map out the key activities to be performed by the sales team to successfully advance to the next step. Key elements of the customer-aligned sales process should include not only these internal activities, but also the customer evidence, that is, outcomes that can be supported by evidence from the customer's perspective showing the activity and sales step have been completed successfully. For example, one high technology company we know was measuring the number of proposals submitted as a key milestone in its sales process and funnel, but it wasn't verifying that the customer (and specifically the decision makers and approvers) had validated the company's solution and value proposition. This resulted in a low win rate and unacceptable cost of sales since most proposals took significant company resources to create.

- *Sales Methods.* There are many third-party solutions in the marketplace that cover different sales models (examples include MHI Global's Strategic Selling®, TAS Group's Target Account Selling™, Holden™, and Challenger™ from the Sales Executive Council) that provide standard frameworks, tools, and a common language to use when planning for accounts and opportunities. Increasingly, we find companies are building their own tools and using the money that they would have spent on third-party tools for coaching and reinforcement to help drive adoption of their overall sales transformation.

- *CRM.* Almost all sales organizations leverage a sales force automation (SFA) or customer relationship management (CRM) tool, whether it's a basic tool such as Act! or an enterprise deployment of Salesforce.com. Regarding sales transformation, this means that companies are not starting from scratch; typically, they have technology in place that may or may not be enabling or valuable to their sales teams. Two questions to consider as you assess your current and future states:

  ○ Is your technology positioned to reinforce your future state—from sales strategy to customer enablement to sales reporting? If not, you should be looking to reassess your must-have requirements or user stories.

  ○ What business questions are being asked that technology could help with? Technology can be critical to your transformation effort, especially from a metrics and tracking perspective. As we've pointed out, technology isn't transformation, but it can help you drive scale and improve sales effectiveness. If technology is the first area you focus on in a sales transformation, you're probably offtrack. We've seen acquisitive companies that end up with five different CRM systems and no holistic view of the pipeline or sales organization because of the disparate technologies that aren't integrated or linked. A lot of CRM implementations fail because they are led by IT and not aligned with the strategy and requirements of the business.

One client we worked with wanted to enable more collaboration across its key regions. Like many global companies, the client's regional operations (EMEA, APAC, Americas, etc.) often functioned as independent entities with separate systems, processes, and standards. But now the chief operating officer (COO) wanted a single view of the global pipeline. As part of the organization's strategy to better engage with its global customer base in an integrated and uniform manner, the client wanted to implement a single CRM system to drive standard business processes in each of the regions. Not surprisingly, the effort met with initial resistance from the regions and countries, but with the COO's sponsorship and drive, the global system was rolled out successfully in less than four months. Although each region still reported separately on its business and performance, the COO now had a global view of the pipeline and could see opportunities to better sell to and service the company's global customers. The overall account planning process changed as well and became more collaborative with global and regional account managers working together and technology making that process change possible.

The maturity or readiness checklist shown in table 5.2 is a quick outline of the key areas to assess as you map out this step and builds on your assessment in the area of sales strategy and structure (see table 5.1).

*Checklist Scenario:*

Many of our clients give their companies a score 1, 2, or 3 on having a defined buyer-aligned sales process. The buyer is rarely thought of in terms of the sales process, and many sellers are taking orders rather than really selling the company's value. The process and tool area checklist gets at the root of a lot of basic elements of an effective sales team: selling processes, planning, and enabling technologies. Many of the elements have dependencies in that it's rare for a client to have high levels of CRM adoption and engagement without a well-defined and implementable buyer-aligned

**Table 5.2** Maturity or Readiness Checklist for Processes and Tools

| # | Implementation Area | Rating (1–10) |
|---|---|---|
| 1 | Buyer-Aligned Sales Process | |
| 2 | Account/Territory Management Processes | |
| 3 | Sales Execution Methodologies/Processes | |
| 4 | Opportunity Management Processes | |
| 5 | CRM and Enabling Technologies | |
| 6 | Sales Activity Management | |

Rating: 1 = process for area is unclear/undefined; 10 = process for area is defined, documented, and robust.

sales process. Most of the areas on this checklist are interdependent, and it's more likely to see all of them with high scores or all with low scores.

## Enablement and People

As much as the Internet and technology have reshaped sales and the balance of power (based on information) between buyers and sellers, many solution and complex sales still require a personal connection. Once your strategy and processes are aligned, the next step is to determine whether you have the "right" people to execute the sales strategy and processes of your vision for the future. If you are transforming the team from one selling products into one selling solutions, this change will reveal those who have the skills or can learn them through training and development and those who cannot.

Most of the transformational efforts that we've researched resulted in sales team turnover of between 20 and 50 percent. However, we also found that successful sales transformations are ultimately more likely to *increase* the overall number of sales professionals; companies with the highest rates of success experienced an overall increase of the number of salespeople by 11 to 20 percent. This makes intuitive sense; your mix of talent will most likely change during the transformation, if it's ultimately successful and driving growth, this will create the need for more team members. The enablement and people part of your roadmap will need to include sections on recruiting, resizing and retraining the sales force. Many of our clients spend a significant amount of time shifting their sales talent from areas of low growth to areas of high growth, which often require different skill sets.

Michael Conway reinforced the importance of this area: "Focus on the people," he told us. "You always want to have good people, good tools, and good process. However, when forced to choose just one, choose good people. They have a way of overcoming obstacles. I believe that organizations can have meaningful improvement in performance through training and tools, but real change requires a significant turnover in staff." During a sales force transformation a healthy amount of turnover will be necessary. Not everyone will be open to a new way of thinking. You need to assess, decide, and take action. And then, says Mike, "Build it into your on-boarding and build it into your recruitment practices." Everyone we interviewed mentioned that transformations usually lead to some degree of shakeout. But be careful not to create resentment or anxiety among people you want to keep. According to Paul Duval, SVP of Central Garden & Pet, you need to identify and categorize your sales resources in the following four key groups:

- those who are willing and able
- those who are willing and not able
- those who are not willing but are able
- those who are not willing and not able

"The focus must be on the first two groups, with an effort to convert the third. The fourth needs to be exited quickly, which demonstrates your commitment to making transformation stick" says Paul. Focus on the willing and the able, which is typically 80 to 90 percent of your sales force. "That's what you need to be successful going forward."

With the right people in place, the enablement roadmap must include everything that enables the sales team to execute as part of the future vision and aligns the selling efforts with the customer's buying process—especially in an innovative or consultative selling approach. For example, if you are moving to a solution or consultative sales approach, you'd want to know whether marketing is an enabler, so that messages, case studies, and collateral are all synched with the future buyer-aligned sales process. This is a reminder of the critical need to engage marketing early in the sales force transformation. Marketing must provide the sales team with the content and tools required to implement your new way of sales.

Common examples include the following:

- insights and initial value propositions
- discovery questions
- value propositions
- case studies

Finally, in another key form of alignment that links back to a sales transformation lever, HR's strong supporting role in the vision for the future includes developing and updating skills programs and success profiles and providing input into compensation plans. HR also plays a supporting role in evaluating talent during the transition when you can expect turnover of 20 percent or more.

In general, we've found that taking orders for a well-known product takes quite different skills than consultatively selling software or services, for example. The latter requires great discovery skills, the ability to use insights, and strong business and political acumen. When we work with client companies that need to change significantly what sellers are focused on and their mix of skills and capabilities, we see that some sellers are able to shift roles with just a bit of training and support, while others are either unable or unwilling to change.

The maturity or readiness checklist shown in table 5.3 is a quick outline of the key areas to assess as you map out this step and builds upon the previous assessments.

*Checklist Scenario:*

Typically, this is an area where we see wide variation depending on the industry and type of sale. For example, in professional services, having strong knowledge management and discovery processes is essential to the business in terms of scoping work and leveraging reusable content from

**Table 5.3**  Maturity or Readiness Checklist for Enablement and People

| # | Implementation Area | Rating (1–10) |
|---|---------------------|---------------|
| 1 | Talent Management | |
| 2 | Customer-Ready Messaging | |
| 3 | Defined Success Stories | |
| 4 | Core Selling Skills | |
| 5 | Knowledge Management | |
| 6 | Sales Operations | |
| 7 | Onboarding & Training | |

Rating: 1 = process or content for area is unclear/undefined; 10 = process or content for area is defined, documented, and robust.

client to client. We also see many client companies that want to be more advanced in a number of the areas, such as core selling skills or sales operations. In our perspective lever discussed in chapter 2, we highlighted the need to capture the inside-out view from the sales organization, and typically, salespeople will not shy away from strong feedback in these areas.

## *Metrics and Management*

We've all heard the expression, "You can't manage what you don't measure." For the most part it's true, but it also has a few nuances. Sales is a function that is inextricably tied to measurement. For example, did you hit your number? What's your quota attainment? How big is the pipeline? Yet, sales is also about relationships, coaching, engagement, and other intangible areas that are not as easy to measure or count. How well does the team manage the business of sales today? How confident are you in the way you measure sales performance? How well can your sales leaders model, coach, and reinforce sales best practices? While these questions are hard to quantify, they're worth bearing in mind as you determine what you're going to measure. When we describe transformation as part art and part science, this is what we mean. Art can't always be quantified, but it should always be considered.

In terms of management, you need to have the right leadership in place as early as possible in the transformation. After all, you want leaders to participate in the transformation. You want them to be an integral part of the transformative culture you're creating. Changing people can mean changing leaders—especially those who resist transformation. "I should have made the moves on the leadership team sooner than I did," Lisa Fiondella, the former chief customer officer (CCO) at Reed Construction Data told us. "I had a lot of counterproductive activity going on when I was trying to do the transformation."

As Lisa's comments suggest, the active engagement of the sales management team is often the key to a successful and lasting sales transformation. Sales managers has a multiplier effect in that they influence their direct reports, perhaps 8 to 10 sellers and potentially more depending on the sales model. As we've said before, engaging the sales management team early in the transformation process is critical and will yield benefits later on. Creating a standard set of success metrics for the transformation will also help in effectively measuring the performance of the entire management team and may reveal who is not actively engaged.

Installing a sales management excellence discipline, one that defines how you run the business of sales is essential to sustaining the new Way of Sales. That discipline includes tracking KPIs and metrics, evaluating and testing the health of your sales pipeline and key opportunities, delivering accurate forecasts, and coaching the team to improve its sales productivity.

What you measure and how you measure it has a significant impact on the success of your transformation. Our survey indicates that the single best predictor of a successful sales transformation is measuring progress (the second most important is management support/sponsorship). While about 80 percent of the organizations we surveyed saw meaningful results in the first 6 months, the overall transformational effort averaged 12 months, and for many companies sales transformation is an ongoing process. Measurements (especially those of leading indicators that can show progress) are critical to sustain the buy-in and ongoing funding necessary to achieve the vision.

**Table 5.4** Maturity or Readiness Checklist for Metrics and Management

| # | Implementation Area | Rating (1–10) |
|---|---|---|
| 1 | Sales Team Goal/Quota Attainment | |
| 2 | Sales Team Turnover | |
| 3 | Standard Sales Metrics & KPIs | |
| 4 | Standard Sales Reports | |
| 5 | Incentive Compensation | |
| 6 | Performance Management Process | |
| 7 | Sales Management Process/Cadence | |
| 8 | Pipeline Management Process | |
| 9 | Forecasting Process | |
| 10 | Coaching & Development | |

Rating: 1 = process or content for area is unclear/undefined; 10 = process or content for area is defined, documented, and robust.

The maturity or readiness checklist shown in table 5.4 is a quick outline of the key areas to assess as you map out this step and builds upon your prior assessments in the other three areas.

*Checklist Scenario:*

From a management perspective, these checklist areas are critical. We worked with a client company that gave itself a score of 1 or 2 regarding pipeline and forecasting processes. The company's pipeline processes were not robust or standard throughout all business units, and it was hard for senior leadership to determine how the business was really performing. Moreover, if the pipeline management area is problematic, it's likely that the forecasting process is an issue as well because the two areas are closely related. We've also had numerous client companies that have had too many metrics and reports rather than not enough; the former is often the more likely scenario. In that case, having too many metrics is often a sign that the business or unit is not clear on what's really important in driving outcomes, and executives dilute their focus with metrics that don't really matter.

Your assessment of your current reality and your roadmap should start broadly with these four areas and include an analysis to compare your current reality with your vision for the future; this will show you the gaps between the two and suggest how to close them and arrive at your goal in the most timely, efficient manner possible.

## Roadmap Development

A sales transformation roadmap enables everyone in the business to understand how your major sales initiatives and programs are sequenced, when they will occur, and whether there are any relevant dependencies, such as managing supply chain alignment, operational standards, or legal hurdles. Each major roadmap item is likely to have its own project or work plan, but the roadmap is the big picture for the overall sales transformation effort.

Developing a roadmap is both art and science, and the first project on a roadmap might not be the optimal place to start, but you need the map and a place to start to gain momentum, show some value or leverage a window of available funding. We have a recommended sequence for your sales transformation effort as shown in figure 5.3.

As our discussion of the sequence lever in chapter 2, the Way of Sales begins with defining the "what" of the strategy and structure and then goes to the "who" and "how" in terms of processes, tools, and people. Finally, the metrics and management section ultimately wraps around all the areas to ensure continuous improvement throughout the Way of Sales. This sequence would be our standard recommendation, but sometimes there are some quick-win projects that you may want to take on first. One of our clients wanted to start the transformation by optimizing the company's global accounts area as it was such an important part of the firm's business. The head of sales thought the company could show significant value by improving its share of wallet with its top accounts and that this would fund the transformation effort and help to build credibility with the executive team. As it turned out, the head of sales was able to fund the transformation effort, and we did some go-to-market strategy work next, along with some other transformation-oriented projects that refocused the business on large accounts and on selling more holistic and integrated solutions.

**Figure 5.3** Illustrative Way of Sales Roadmap.

Building your sales transformation roadmap is a major effort—a project in itself—that will take time and an investment of resources, not only from your sales team but also from other internal stakeholders (marketing, HR, etc.) as well as from customers. As we stated in chapter 4, including internal stakeholders is a best practice for improving the chance of success of your transformation effort. In terms of customers, it is important to share parts of your roadmap with some key customers to capture their input and feedback. Many customers like to be included and are often appreciative to be asked their opinion and welcome the opportunity to be a strategic partner. For one of our clients, a key customer wanted the company to focus more on product innovation and was willing to help cocreate a new solution with the client. The roadmap included a section on this project that helped to round out the client's product strategy and go-to-market strategy. Other customers were also interested in this new solution, and our client created a small customer advisory board to help craft and shape the company's communications to the market. Including customers as part of your roadmap review can pay significant dividends and help build key customers' loyalty.

In closing, each step of the roadmap should be detailed and will take a significant amount of time to explore and articulate. Analyzing the gap between your current reality and your vision of the future is one of the first steps in your transformation journey, followed by prioritization of gaps, identifying initiatives and programs to close the gaps, and sequencing the right projects to make the transformation happen.

In chapter 6, we'll discuss how to use your roadmap to implement a sales force transformation that's unique to your organization.

### Chapter 5: Building Your Sales Transformation Roadmap—Takeaways

- Your sales transformation roadmap is comprised of the gaps between your current state and your vision for the future. To

| Transformation Area / Phase | Owner | Status | Quarter | | | | | | | |
|---|---|---|---|---|---|---|---|---|---|---|
| | | | 1Q15 | 2Q15 | 3Q15 | 4Q15 | 1Q16 | 2Q16 | 3Q16 | 4Q16 |
| **Strategy & Structure** | | | | | | | | | | |
| Go-to-Market Strategy | | | | | | | | | | |
| Kickoff Meeting | MP | ⇑ | | | | | | | | |
| Voice of the Customer Discovery | WS | ⇔ | | | | | | | | |
| Customer Segmentation Analysis | | | | | | | | | | |
| Sales Force Performance & Workload | | | | | | | | | | |
| Sales Coverage Analysis | | | | | | | | | | |
| Development of GTM Model | | | | | | | | | | |
| Implementation Roadmap | | | | | | | | | | |
| Sales Org Development & Structure | | | | | | | | | | |
| **Processes & Tools** | | | | | | | | | | |
| Sales Process Definition | | | | | | | | | | |
| CRM Readiness/Alignment | | | | | | | | | | |
| Account / Terr / Opp Mgmt. | | | | | | | | | | |
| **Enablement & People** | | | | | | | | | | |
| Define Skills/Competencies | | | | | | | | | | |
| Develop Sales-Ready Messaging | | | | | | | | | | |
| Value Prop Alignment | | | | | | | | | | |
| **Metrics & Management** | | | | | | | | | | |
| Sales Mgmt. Cadence | | | | | | | | | | |
| Scorecard/Dashboard Definition | | | | | | | | | | |
| Sales Coaching Development | | | | | | | | | | |
| **Program Management** | | | | | | | | | | |
| Status Meetings | | | | | | | | | | |
| Program Communications / Metrics | | | | | | | | | | |

**Figure 5.3** Illustrative Way of Sales Roadmap.

Building your sales transformation roadmap is a major effort—a project in itself—that will take time and an investment of resources, not only from your sales team but also from other internal stakeholders (marketing, HR, etc.) as well as from customers. As we stated in chapter 4, including internal stakeholders is a best practice for improving the chance of success of your transformation effort. In terms of customers, it is important to share parts of your roadmap with some key customers to capture their input and feedback. Many customers like to be included and are often appreciative to be asked their opinion and welcome the opportunity to be a strategic partner. For one of our clients, a key customer wanted the company to focus more on product innovation and was willing to help cocreate a new solution with the client. The roadmap included a section on this project that helped to round out the client's product strategy and go-to-market strategy. Other customers were also interested in this new solution, and our client created a small customer advisory board to help craft and shape the company's communications to the market. Including customers as part of your roadmap review can pay significant dividends and help build key customers' loyalty.

In closing, each step of the roadmap should be detailed and will take a significant amount of time to explore and articulate. Analyzing the gap between your current reality and your vision of the future is one of the first steps in your transformation journey, followed by prioritization of gaps, identifying initiatives and programs to close the gaps, and sequencing the right projects to make the transformation happen.

In chapter 6, we'll discuss how to use your roadmap to implement a sales force transformation that's unique to your organization.

### Chapter 5: Building Your Sales Transformation Roadmap—Takeaways

- Your sales transformation roadmap is comprised of the gaps between your current state and your vision for the future. To craft your roadmap, you'll need to outline both states and determine specific, measurable ways to close the gaps.

- Our experience and our research have shown that the more detailed a gap analysis, the greater the chance of a successful sales force transformation. In some cases, the gap analysis itself may take several weeks to complete. Avoid skipping steps.

- Successful transformations occur throughout four main areas of sales capability and effectiveness: sales strategy and structure, processes and tools, enablement and people, and metrics and management. We call these four areas the Way of Sales.

- The Way of Sales starts with defining the "what" of the strategy and structure and then goes on to the "who" and "how" of processes, tools, and people. Metrics and management wrap around all four areas to ensure continuous improvement.

# CHAPTER 6

## Implementing Your Sales Transformation

At this point in your sales transformation journey, you have assembled your reports and your analyses; you've gotten buy-in from your sales team, other internal functional teams, and the C-suite. You know what transformation will require. Now it's time to begin to implement your strategy. At this juncture, you are ready to move through implementation and your roadmap to close the gaps you have identified and to achieve your vision.

There is no shortage of clichés and platitudes about implementation. "This is where the rubber meets the road" and similar expressions exist for a reason: implementation is where you make your mark. You've built your case for change, your vision, and your roadmap. Now it's time to put it all into practice. Even with the "best" roadmap, you'll still need to be flexible. One of our mentors, Bill Frank, was a captain in the United States Army and flew helicopters in the Vietnam War. A highly decorated pilot who was twice awarded the Distinguished Flying Cross, Bill was one of the first to pilot the Apache attack helicopter. One of our favorite quotes from Bill, and there are many, refers to the disconnect we often experience between a plan and reality. As he told us many times based on hard-earned experience, "When the map and the terrain differ, go with the terrain."

Fortunately for us, a sales transformation doesn't carry nearly the same impact or consequences, but the lesson applies: your roadmap will shape your overall effort, but you must adjust and allow for changes along the way. Your business, customers, and competitors are not standing around and waiting for you to transform, and your salespeople still need to perform during this time in order to meet their own goals and achieve their incentives.

Essentially, a sales force transformation centers on people: salespeople, sales support, customers, competitors, and even vendors and suppliers. All of the structure, processes, tools, compensation, training, and metrics are designed to enable your organization to have a unique and value-added conversation with your customers.

At Central Garden & Pet, the ability to have a differentiated conversation in a complex consumer goods market was critical to the success of a two-phase sales transformation in the pet division. Both of these sales force transformations involved consolidations of several sales forces that had originated from a series of acquisitions. Each of the separate sales teams were selling to different categories in the pet market. The transformations were designed to do three things:

1. reduce sales costs
2. enable broader, more strategic business conversations about driving the larger pet business
3. make it easier for customers to do business with Central

The first transformation involved determining how to integrate sales teams from five business units. Each unit was comprised of a team of product specialists who were experts in selling their unique product offerings. The sales transformation vision was to integrate these divisions into one unit that would drive more efficiencies and increase earnings while also delivering more value to retailer customers. In the current state, the retailers often had to sit through numerous—and sometimes overlapping—product-focused conversations with several salespeople from Central, rather than having broader business discussions about how Central could help them drive overall performance.

## *Sales Transformation at Central Garden & Pet*

The transformation began with an analysis of the customer base, the small and medium independent pet stores in the United States, to determine the amount of sales coverage and capacity required to serve these customers effectively and efficiently. In terms of sales coverage, Central set specific goals for revenues by store and customer satisfaction; regarding sales capacity, Central wanted to reduce the cost of selling to those customers by 10 percent. This analysis required examining the amount of time spent selling and servicing customers of various sizes as well as the location of these customers to identify the number of salespeople required to optimize returns with the integrated team of the future.

In addition to this inside-out analysis, we also looked at the outside-in perspective through a voice of the customer (VOC) analysis with several customers to understand what they wanted from Central; this would help to drive the types of sales conversations the sellers should be having. This insight was critical to keeping the transformation externally focused on the customer, and it aided the change management efforts. Even though there were opportunities to reduce selling costs, the leadership team was able to focus the transformation message on meeting customer needs, a much more powerful motivator for change in the organization.

Once the appropriate sales coverage was determined, we then worked to determine the future sales roles:

- Territory Manager: covering a set of small to midsized customers in a defined geographic location
- Account Manager: covering a specific set of larger accounts
- Sales Manager: the first-level leader overseeing a team of territory or account managers

As we discussed in chapter 2 with the lever of alignment, we worked closely with the human resources department to help define the desired future competencies required for success in each of these roles. Engaging HR was critical to ensure that we helped Central make the right resourcing decisions for both current employees and new hires, and it also ensured that we didn't vary from any core HR principles that might be impacted by the transformation.

We found that several basic sales competencies would be taken over from the current situation into the desired future one. For example, the territory managers would need to be able to prioritize the customers in their area and map their routes and activities accordingly, a common task of field salespeople covering a geographic area. Overall, however, we realized that some of the new competency requirements for individual sellers would drive the initiative's success. Essentially, these salespeople would now need to communicate and manage across several broad categories as opposed to dealing with a single specialty. This change meant that they needed to know how to sell without necessarily being an expert on everything in their bag. In order to accomplish this change, the sellers needed to develop stronger skills working with others in the organization who could provide more specialized expertise as needed. These salespeople also needed to know how to have broader business discussions that would enable them to sell solutions rather than individual products. Selling solutions often requires learning how to develop more senior-level relationships in your customers' organization, relationships that require a different level of conversation and overall level of care and feeding.

We now had defined the future roles and structure to support the vision—an integrated team bringing the full breadth of products and category insights to the customers. But who could fill these roles? How many of the current sales team members would be successful in this future sales model? In what capacity? Did we need all members of the existing teams? With the help of the current sales leadership team and the human resources department, we facilitated a process to evaluate the current team and compare it to the desired future organizational structure. We helped the team determine where there would be gaps that would be filled through recruiting and where current team members who were not a fit would either need to find other roles within Central or leave the company. We assigned the current sales leadership team the task of stack-ranking the current sales team based on recent sales performance and an assessment of the individual in view of the future role and competencies. In order to ensure that the team members had the support they needed for this task, which was largely out of their day-to-day comfort zone, we facilitated the process over two days of hard work. Ultimately, this exercise produced a list of the current team members mapped to future roles.

While we coordinated with the human resources department on the individual team changes, we began development of the sales processes as well as tools and training that would be rolled out to this team at a launch meeting. This work included some updates to the Central Way of Sales, which had been deployed previously, and coordination with the brand teams to design sales collateral and product training to equip the sales team to present the "full bag" to customers. Lastly, we also developed several customer planning tools to enable the territory managers to prioritize their accounts, their time, and their schedule to maximize their productivity.

We brought the new integrated pet sales team together in Atlanta for a three-day launch meeting with objectives that included:

- communicating expectations for the new team and sales roles
- preparing the teams to position and sell the full portfolio of Central Garden & Pet branded products
- building camaraderie and alignment with the new team
- developing territory and account plans based on the revised customer assignments

Once launched, the sales team had an immediate impact on customers and Central's results. Even though Central's business has struggled overall in the past couple of years, this independent pet sales team was a success and achieved an increase of more than 20 percent in revenues after the first year while saving more than $2 million in sales costs.

### Step 6: Implementing a Sales Force Transformation

Most successful sales transformations that we've been a part of or have researched have generally followed a similar implementation path (step

6 in our overall sales transformation process) to the one we described for Central:

1. Get the right sales leader(s) in place and involve them throughout implementation.
2. Update/modify the sales strategy and structure.
3. Get the right people into the right roles
4. Deploy processes and tools to enable your future team.
5. Measure and communicate results.
6. Iterate based on results—move into another phase (if required).

Each of these components is designed to optimize your team. As we discussed in chapter 2, one of the key levers for your sales transformation is first focusing on the "what" of sales strategy and structure and then on the "who" of people and enablement. At this point, you should have already determined your needs. Now your implementation will focus on a key subset of people: your sales leaders who share your vision and will lead the sales teams in the future.

### Get the Right Leaders in Place

In many of our interviews for this book, getting the right leadership in place was mentioned as an almost universal factor for success. A strong sales transformation leader must have empathy for the sales team as well as for the customers. Jim Dougherty echoed these comments: "What's counterintuitive is a lot of leaders believe they are put in place because they are smart and successful and they know what they're doing; they have the answers. I traveled nonstop to meet sales reps and support people all over the world, and as opposed to having the answer, I'd ask them questions." The right leadership applies at the highest levels of your organization says Eileen Martinson, CEO of Sparta Systems in an interview. "When you're transforming, a CEO has to engage," she says. "And it's not just the sales organization. You have to transform the way you sell and think about customers and value across the entire company."

So who is the "right" leader for a transformation? As the title of the bestselling book by Marshall Goldsmith, *What Got You Here Won't Get You There,*[1] suggests, sometimes a leader managing the status quo may not be the right person to lead a transformation. While empathy is a key quality, there's more. A transformational leader needs to be able to make hard decisions, especially about people. Sometimes this involves drastically changing the perspective of many individuals, and a transformational leader needs to be confident enough in her own vision that she can make uncompromising decisions that chart the path forward. While making these tough decisions, this leader also needs to know how to effectively paint the vision for her team members, help them see the value, help them accept the change, and help them to understand how to implement the vision. At the same time, this leader needs to keep the business functioning and minimize any potential negative effects on customers.

For example, we worked with a major financial services firm to design a new organizational structure and territory alignment for a team that manages significant account relationships. In order to grow these accounts while reducing account attrition, account managers needed to bring better insights and have more value-based conversations with their clients. These objectives were difficult in the current environment because the account managers covered a variety of industries and were geographically dispersed, making face-to-face meetings with clients challenging and costly. Our proposed new sales structure more tightly aligned the sales team with specific industries and geographies.

On paper, everyone was on board with this new structure. The theory behind it was sound, and the benefits were obvious. However, this alignment required that most account managers turn over 80 to 90 percent of their current portfolio. Needless to say, when we presented the new territories and showed the specific changes to the leader of this group, there was a long pause on the other end of the phone. Our client's first inclination was to immediately start backpedaling. He was fearful and worried about the change he had just committed to implement, and his empathy with his people and his clients was giving him second thoughts about the change.

Once our client got over his initial shock and refocused on his vision, he realized that he needed to move forward with some hard decisions. He set about making sure that he had the information he needed so that he could have informed conversations with each member of his team about what the new reality would look like. He collaborated with the human resources department before each of these conversations. His goal was to paint the picture of what each new role would encompass, why it was so vital to the success of the organization, and what the value would be to each individual and client in the new structure.

This leader arrived at a critical conclusion: He realized that not every decision needed to be his own. He set the vision, and then he engaged his direct reports to help make decisions about how they would tactically structure their responsibilities. He felt strongly about empowering his team to make decisions and drive change, even if those decisions weren't perfectly aligned with what he would do. Most research finds that great sales leaders are masters at developing and motivating talent, and they need to let their people fail and learn.

### Update Your Sales Strategy and Structure

The purpose of any sales transformation should be to improve your ability to successfully execute a winning sales strategy that will drive results for your organization. The sales structure shouldn't inhibit sales or negatively impact the customers' experience. For example, in the case of Central Garden & Pet, the strategy was to drive a larger share of the business with pet stores by selling integrated solutions. This strategy was based on customer feedback and the market opportunity of owning a greater share of customer shelf space. We knew that we needed to integrate the sales teams in order to help Central execute this strategy, but we also knew that we needed to equip the salespeople to effectively execute the sales process. The salespeople needed to come up to speed quickly and be able to position offerings from a large portfolio. They also needed to start connecting with specialists in the organization to drive results in particular categories or for targeted opportunities. To this end, we also needed to make sure that the sales leadership structure could support the new sales process and that it was operating in a manner that supported the ultimate strategy and sales objectives.

The next people consideration occurs when you define your new organization structure and then map existing roles to roles that will support your new strategy and structure. In order to do this effectively, you will need to map out the future organization and then begin to define details for each of the roles. These details should include the following:

- *Workload analysis* to ensure that you have enough staff to effectively execute your strategy and meet your objectives and to ensure that individuals in the future roles can meet expectations and be successful in their new roles.
- *Descriptions of future roles and expectations* that clearly define both the qualities of the ideal candidate for the role as well as the tasks of the individual in the role must accomplish to be successful based on your vision and on the type of conversations your team should have with customers.
- *Plan for future career path* to outline what the expected development path is for employees in each of the roles.
- *Future compensation model* to define exactly how individuals in the new roles will be compensated on both a fixed and variable basis and how those variables align with the expectations outlined for the roles.

Your sales strategy and structure will reflect the vision that you have established for your sales force and for the type of conversations your team will conduct with your customers. In many cases where the driver of a sales force transformation is to integrate an acquisition or convert from a portfolio of companies to a portfolio of brands, the task is to deploy a structure that will promote a team-selling concept and allow for more thorough and coordinated customer engagement. This often requires a new set of skills. Once you have updated your strategy and structure on paper, it is time to fill the organization charts with the people that will implement your sales strategy.

### *Get the Right People in Place*

Ultimately, it's the people who will determine the success or failure of your transformation. This includes the people who will design and drive your transformation forward as well as the people who will be affected by and have to change as a result of your transformation. Within this context, we think of people across several dimensions: sales team, first-level sales leaders, sales operations and support, and your transformation team—typically a mix of insiders and outside specialists.

During your transformation, you need to consider individuals from four primary groups:

- *Project Team:* A group that is dedicated solely to the transformation's design and implementation. In most cases, this should include insiders as well as individuals who can bring an outside, objective perspective. Insiders on this team will have been taken out of their day jobs for temporary assignment on the transformation team. This dedicated team is critical. As a leader, you need to ensure that as many of your team members as possible can maintain their focus on business as usual and keep the business running while transformation planning takes place. At the same time, you don't want transformation planning to take a backseat because everyone's time is devoted to day-to-day operations.

- *Business as Usual:* These individuals may or may not have knowledge of the transformation until it's time for them to make the change. In some cases they may participate in brief interviews or other events conducted by the transformation team, but they are generally spending 90 to 95 percent of their days running the business. It's important to keep as many individuals as possible in this position until change is required.

- *Hybrids:* These are the individuals who play a larger role in the transformation but also maintain day-to-day responsibilities. They are generally the primary connection point between the transformation team and the realities in the field; their feedback about what will and won't work is typically invaluable as they bring a pragmatic viewpoint to the table. Their level of involvement may vary from part-time to serving on a steering committee or functioning in the role of subject matter expert. It's critical to carefully consider who should be members in this group for the following reasons:

- They may find themselves stretched for time and attention given their dual roles. Therefore, it's especially important that they are engaged when their input and participation is most valuable.
- They might not always be objective in their feedback because they are more apt to look at each change through the lens of how it will affect their specific role. This becomes extremely critical to note if their role will substantially change or be eliminated in the new structure.
- They may leak communication to the field either intentionally or inadvertently.

- *Outside Supporters*: This includes the human resources department, which is a valuable partner to the sales team both during and after a sales force transformation. Human resources can provide expertise on how to shift people, change their roles, and transition them in and out of the organization. However, when working through a sales force transformation and assessing future talent requirements, we've found that it's important to use the human resources department as a facilitator while ensuring that sales is heavily involved in the details of the transition (such as role descriptions, training, and hiring requirements). Other supporting groups may include IT if a technology change will accompany the transformation. Overall it's important to ensure that sales does not fully outsource the function of these supporting groups to a third party that isn't equipped with the necessary deep knowledge of the sales function.

Once you have identified these groups, you'll need to develop an objective, structured plan to determine how to move from the status quo to the desired future. While some choices are obvious, it's important to make sure that all decisions about personnel changes and moves can be justified based on role descriptions and qualifications. In order to do this, we recommend the development of an employee information template that summarizes for each employee his or her most recent performance, leadership potential, years of experience, and potential in regard to the future role. In many cases, it's key to involve a leader who is familiar with each of the individuals who will be transitioned to include feedback based on direct observations.

At Central Garden & Pet, a full-day facilitated session with the sales leaders of each of the groups was designed. In preparation for the session, we had the sales leaders complete the employee transition templates. We then presented the new structure, described the roles for each level, and reviewed each employee's qualifications for the new roles. In this case, a very formal process was critical as this transformation involved the termination of employees as well as significant shifts in titles and responsibilities.

With another client, a Fortune 1000 financial services firm, the new sales structure resulted in net neutral head count. However, there were significant role changes in terms of types and sizes of accounts to be managed as well as responsibility for managing people, something we often found in our survey of sales transformations. In this case, the leader of the group identified some of the senior employees whom he wanted to position for new roles and had conversations with them prior to completing the organization structure. Before these conversations, he spoke at length with the transformation team and with the human resources department to ensure he understood the implications of what he was offering in terms of responsibilities, expectations, and compensation changes. Once those roles were in place, we began to consider the other roles where the expectations did not change as drastically from the current to the future state. In these cases, we helped make decisions based on minimizing change to customer portfolios and lessening the impact on the overall customer experience.

There are many more formalized tools that can be used to assess salespeople's competency and their potential for aligning with the roles in your new structure. In addition, there are a number of ways to approach this discussion with the transformation team. We have seen companies post new roles and ask existing team members to self-assess or "apply" for the new positions. We have also seen companies leverage external assessments focused on sales roles from firms such as Chally and Caliper that can provide an additional perspective on the fit of an individual for the future sales roles.

After defining the desired future and comparing your current situation to it, you can use a business impact analysis to chart the next steps in the transition by exploring the following questions:

- How will specific roles be affected—for example, changes in responsibility, changes in customer base, changes in compensation, etc.?
- How will salespeople's behavior be impacted by role changes, and how might that affect sales and the customer experience?
- How might customers be affected? Are there risks? What is the communication plan? What is the risk mitigation strategy?

Of course, as you look at your business impact analysis, make sure that you consider the human element, namely, your sales team. As Don Perry told us, "You have lots of opinions, lots of stages; 20 percent will buy it, 60 percent will move toward it and 20 percent will never get it at all. You've got to understand your audience and what you're trying to achieve."

## Deploy Processes, Tools, and Enablement

Once your new structure is defined and you have identified the leaders and salespeople who will comprise the future team, it's time to outline the processes that your team will use to successfully execute your new strategy. Make sure that these processes cover all of the critical connection points with you, your team, your customers, your partners, and other areas of your organization. Generally, when you outline processes, they begin to look like a chain of boxes and arrows, but keep in mind that this is not the way that your sales team will most effectively absorb this information. It's critical to shape the processes into content that your salespeople can absorb. Checklists, templates, and simple field guides can be highly effective tools in supporting these processes.

Similarly, make sure that your technology enablers support your new processes or at least be sure that you can clearly communicate any disconnects and needed work-arounds. Finally, ensure that you have the right reinforcement plan in place to make your rollout an ongoing reality, not just a one-time event.

At Central Garden & Pet, new processes were rolled out to company's sales and merchandising teams. These teams were usually in and out of hardware stores all day long. They lived in their trucks and could often be found toting around sample bags of seeds and lawn chemicals. Much of our process rollout concentrated on improving how they planned and executed sales calls at their customers' stores, so we wanted to make sure they were equipped with the right tools and references to have at their fingertips. We also knew that we needed tools that could survive in their office environment for more than a week. We outlined about 15 key concepts that we wanted to reinforce, and then we had those concepts printed on hard plastic cards that were held together on a key ring. As we worked with the team and their leaders in the field, we found these key rings everywhere—hooked to laptop bags and belt buckles and sitting in the passenger seats. They became part of the planning process for sales calls and continued to reinforce the key concepts we had rolled out.

At other organizations, we have rolled out meeting cadence guides for sales managers that include plans for regular meetings, such as annual planning, quarterly reviews, and weekly pipeline calls, as well as coaching points for each meeting. We have generally produced these as thin spiral-bound tools that can easily ride along in a laptop bag, but we've also produced them in electronic form so that they can be viewed easily on a laptop or tablet.

In general, we find that it's more important to align the tools with the reality of the salesperson rather than to find the slickest, most innovative solution. These tools must be part of the day-to-day routine in the way that is most practical for each salesperson, and they need to be simple to use and easy to reference. As with technology enablers and templates, these tools should enable the process, not detract from its execution. When designing input forms, whether for technology or document-based templates, make sure that what you require facilitates the process and balance your requirements with what the salesperson really needs to think through or record in order to be more effective in executing your sales strategy. Keep in mind that no one sells anything by filling in a template. Therefore, that work should be minimal and have a profitable outcome.

At a financial services technology company, we successfully rolled out a new win-planning process, and we enabled this process with a very simple template in Microsoft Word that had high-level categories, thought-provoking questions, and a great deal of white space that could be filled in with the appropriate level of detail depending on the size of the deal. This win-plan template explored the top 30 questions that sales leaders ask their team members about every one of their high-level deals. The win plan was part of a playbook that provided a unified vision for the program, clarified role definitions, and established an operating model. It also created account cadence plans, defined a system for account visioning/joint customer planning, set guidelines for account reviews/portfolio management, and laid the foundation for opportunity management. One example of this program's success was reported by a regional sales leader whose team had underperformed in the previous two years. As a result of adopting this process, he was able to exceed his team goal by 169 percent and increase the number of team members achieving their individual goals to 100 percent.

### Measure and Communicate Results

Because transformations often occur gradually over a period of time and because sales results can derive from a variety of internal and external factors, it's important for you to lay out specific metrics that will help you to understand if your transformation has in fact achieved its established objectives. These measures should be balanced to consider sales results alongside other objectives you had hoped to achieve, such as improving specific customer satisfaction metrics, reducing sales employee turnover, or reducing sales costs.

Communicating success to the organization involves several different elements. Obviously, you want to report to senior leadership that their investments are yielding results. It's critical to ensure that you have the resources for any upcoming initiatives you wish to pursue. However, there is another dimension that you'll want to be very careful not to overlook: communicating progress to your team. Behavior change takes time and requires positive reinforcement along the way. Regular communication to your team about how its participation in the change is driving results will go a long way to getting and keeping team members on board with your vision.

During the transformations we have led, we have structured specific types of follow-up communications. They may be delivered via email, video, staff calls, distance learning modules, or other forms of communication that are appropriate for the message being delivered and the audience receiving it. These communication types include the following:

- reinforcement reminders about processes and best practices
- success stories that highlight specific individuals or teams that are achieving success with the new sales model
- team results that show incremental improvement and what the impact will be for the organization, for customers, and for the salespeople
- recognition of individuals or teams who are embracing the change and achieving results

During a transformation we led at a large hospitality organization, we placed all of the supporting training content, tools, and templates on a centralized portal, and we created a series of monthly reinforcement "skill builders" that transformation champions could use with their teams to begin using the content the portal made available to them. These skill builders were essentially the structured outline and key messaging that champions could use to coach their teams with a specific focus each month on a skill that was relevant during that particular business cycle. By doing this, we also enabled champions to better understand the skills required so that they could recognize individual successes in their regions. These success stories were posted to the portal and became examples so that users could continue to better understand how to drive results with the new sales processes.

### Iterate Based on Results

Making dramatic changes successful can take a long time. In the equity markets or private equity world it's all about return on investment. Many studies have shown that it takes anywhere from 24 to 48 days to change a habit—and that's if you're motivated to change it! Combine that with the fact that, in most cases, salespeople need to first absorb and accept the change and then figure out how to make it part of what they do. Then add the fact that many of them will need coaching in order to transform what they do into something they do effectively. And all of this occurs while business is changing and evolving. This is why incremental, balanced measures are important and why it is important to keep a finger on the pulse of change at all levels.

In some cases, no matter how many people are involved in designing the change, you just don't know what you don't know until you find out that, well, you didn't know it after all. This happens in almost every transformation. The key to overcoming these bumps in the road is to try not to let it happen too often and minimize the impact as soon as you find out. Make sure to keep your ears to the ground at all levels and be sure that you keep at least part of your transformation team intact for a defined period of time after you start to implement.

We worked with one client to help the company's sellers complete opportunity plans in preparation for deal reviews with their managers. In doing so, we learned a few things about the transformation. First, it became apparent that many skill gaps had not been addressed through the transformation. Many of the senior salespeople not only struggled to define the opportunity, but they lacked the knowledge of how to effectively navigate to the right contacts in the organization—and they struggled to define effective win themes. Second, we learned that the sales organization's structure was inhibiting salespeople's ability to focus on big deals because they needed significant support in qualifying a larger number of leads being generated. As a result of these findings, we were able to begin working with the client to improve the training materials available to the group and to make additional structural adjustments that provided greater support for qualifying leads early in the funnel. At the same time, we helped bring the appropriate subject matter expertise to opportunities that emerged in the later stages of the sales funnel.

### Summary

We often see clients who spend the majority of their transformation budget designing the ultimate transformation and accompanying processes, tools, and technology. They easily underestimate the time and energy required to actually implement the transformation and affect real change within their organization. As a result, they may add another bell or whistle to the design instead of allotting part of the budget for implementation.

When you plan your transformation, understand that implementation itself is a process and real behavior change takes more than a kickoff meeting or webinar.

### Chapter 6: Implementing Your Sales Transformation—Takeaways

- While planning and talking is part of the transformation process, implementation is where you make your mark.
- A well-defined future state supports your vision for sales force transformation.
- It's key to coordinate implementation with the human resources department and with any other internal functional areas, such as IT, that are affected by the transformation.

- While every organization is unique, we've found that sales forces that implement right tend to dedicate resources to updating/modifying the sales strategy and structure; get the right people in place in the right roles; deploy processes, tools, and enablement to prepare your future team; measure and communicate results; and then iterate based on the results.

# CHAPTER 7

# Key Barriers and Considerations for Implementation

N ow that you're beginning the process of implementing your own sales transformation, let's review several potential barriers to success. This list is not exhaustive, but like the levers outlined in chapter 2, these items apply almost universally when significant change and transformation are carried out in a sales organization. We have compiled the list from and our interviews with sales executives our own experiences that involve more than 100 transformations—some successful, others not—and in each case, one or more of these barriers were crucial for the outcome. Experience and hindsight can be great teachers. Many of the executives we interviewed indicated that they discovered these barriers only during or after transformation, not before. Our aim is to help you succeed by equipping you with these insights as you are planning and launching your sales force transformation.

## *Key Barriers*

In a sales force transformation, barriers may obstruct the progress of one or more of the core people, processes, or technology elements. Typically, these are not physical barriers, but issues of position, leverage, or sequence. Take technology and sales tools as an example: A company will often implement a technology tool by saying, "Now we're using the latest tool." The good news is that the new tool is flexible; the bad news is that it's flexible. If you've got people thinking about technology in different directions, the only thing that you'll automate is chaos. This explains why you may be having a lot of problems with your sales force automation tool, and these can prevent your changes from becoming common practice. This is one of many barriers you may face during your sales force transformation.

### Success as a Barrier to Success

Many sales organizations that achieve strong results today may be in trouble in the future because it's hard to build momentum for a sales transformation when things are going well. This brings to mind Jim Collins's idea: "Good is the enemy of great."[1] Sure, riding a market "wave" can be exhilarating, but it can also be a barrier to making the changes necessary to succeed when the market turns—as it will. Boom-and-bust cycles happen in every industry. As venture capitalist Marc Andreessen posted on Twitter, "When the market turns, and it will turn, we will find out who has been swimming without trunks on."[2] Sales organizations that don't adapt will not be successful going forward.

This barrier exists both at the beginning of a transformation when you are building your case for change and throughout your implementation when you are overcoming the status quo. As Allison Montgomery, a sales enablement executive at Deluxe Corporation, told us during an interview, "If your sales results are positive or good enough, having the runway to make transformative changes that will set you up for success in the long haul will be very difficult. Why make those changes when you are doing well? You can get stuck. Success is a barrier to success." When you begin to see positive results from your sales force transformation, make sure not to allow institutional momentum to divert you from your vision and original objectives. In many industries, competitive advantage is built and sustained not by what you are selling, but how. Avoid the temptation to be satisfied with "good enough."

## Keeping the Lights On

Being a sales leader is a tenuous role. Your performance is easily measured, and you are expected to "see around corners" to prepare for market shifts and changes without putting current revenue at risk. The classic adage of changing the tire while the car is moving applies here. Many people we have worked with were bullish on a sales transformation effort until they lost a significant deal or a major customer defected. Often it was a deal they should have lost or a customer who was not ideal, but nevertheless the reality of keeping the lights on and achieving short-term targets is very salient to the sales organization. Which is why having the entire organization on board for the mission is so important.

We also observed this barrier at a Fortune 100 technology company where we needed to get the sales team, frontline sales managers, and vice presidents thinking not only about meeting sales goals, but also about adding new people and products and changing into a more solution-oriented sales force—all at the same time. This was further complicated by the fact that some of the sales teams operated under monthly quotas.

## Technology / Data Complexity

Most customers we talk to today are thinking of, moving to, or already leveraging cloud technologies to run their businesses. The rise of Salesforce.com is a strong testament to the power of the cloud for front-office transformation. The dirty little secret, however, is that all the old systems, applications, and databases are often still running in the background to keep the lights on. A lot of companies don't decommission old systems, and too much time is spent reconciling "the numbers" between the different reports, systems, and analyses. In some cases, managers keep track of their forecasts in Excel spreadsheets on the side.

As Paul Duval told us in an interview, "People think, 'If we could just add computers, sales should go up.' Companies rely on software solutions, but at the end of the day they are just enablers. The salesperson still has to sell. Don't rely on the great computer to be the be-all." This sentiment was echoed by many other leaders including Eileen Martinson, the CEO of Sparta Systems, a software company with more than 650,000 users in thirty countries. "At the end of the day, technology is a means to an end," she said during our conversation. "If you can create the value proposition and get out of the shiny new object mode, that's the most important thing. We don't' focus on the technology. We focus on the value proposition." This perspective applies both internally to the use of technology and tools in a sales transformation as well as externally when positioning your solutions with customers.

### Your Problems "Walk and Talk"

There is a saying that within many companies the "people make the place." Working with talented, motivated, and authentic people is truly a joy, but everyone knows that there is a subset of people who can make a sales transformation harder. The naysayers, the skeptics, and the passive-aggressive head nodders, among others, can be a real barrier to moving fast and realizing quick wins.

In a massive study of 7,600 managers in 262 companies across 30 industries highlighted in the *Harvard Business Review*, "Why Strategy Execution Unravels—and What to Do About It,"[3] the researchers found that only 9 percent of managers said they could rely on colleagues in other functions and units all the time, and just half of the respondents said they could rely on them most of the time. As we've stated elsewhere in this book, being able to create cross-functional coalitions and alliances throughout the business is a significant factor in having a successful sales transformation. In the study previously cited, when managers were asked about the single greatest challenge to executing their company's strategy, 30 percent cited failure to coordinate across units. In our own survey of more than a hundred sales leaders, our research corroborated that people challenges and cross-functional coordination were some of the biggest barriers to sales transformation success.

While these barriers are not insignificant, they are predictable. And they can be addressed by elements of your roadmap and implementation plan based on your assessment of your company, culture, timing, and desired outcomes from your sales transformation. Marriott was once famous for training its hotel staff with a customer orientation of: "The answer is 'yes,' now what is the question?" In consulting, the answer often is "it depends." This applies to your sales transformation in which your approach, experience, and outcome will be specific to your organization.

## Key Considerations

Next, let's look at some key considerations for your implementation process, many of which will help you overcome or even avoid these barriers.

## Pilot When Possible

Most people agree that a trial is usually a good idea, especially for larger commitments. It's like test-driving a car before deciding whether to buy it, or obtaining references and a background check on a new employee, or getting an appraisal and an inspection before purchasing a home. Testing the key elements of your sales transformation roadmap can pay off in several ways, such as increasing your understanding of areas to refine and capturing result metrics that can be leveraged to secure funding and buy-in for the full deployment. Earlier, we mentioned how Everett Hill helped a major bottling company understand that distribution also needed to transform in order to support customer expectations and, ultimately, the sales transformation. Reflecting on his approach during our interview with him, he said, "I would start with a pilot and scale it business unit by business unit to build credibility and momentum." Because of the confidence and results gained through the initial pilot, Everett was able to "sell" the transformation to other regions. "When I introduced the change initiative in Florida," he told us, "a director of sales—with 40 sales reps in his organization—gets 6 inches from my face, and he says 'I've been here in Orlando for 20 years and distribution has been screwed up for 20 years. I don't care what you do with sales; you have to make distribution effective.'" Everett asked for 90 days to transform distribution. The director agreed. "After 90 days he couldn't believe the ability we had to deliver to our customers. And he said, 'Sign me up for sales transformation!'"

The concept of a pilot was a consistent theme through most of the successful sales transformations we've studied and worked on. Pilots typically start with a small group or division testing, refining, and gaining real-world proof from within the company; then the group leverages the experience and results to scale across the sales organization. The pilot directly supports the internal sales campaign discussed in chapter 4. It's like providing a proof of concept when you're selling to a Fortune 500 company. And like a proof of concept with a prospect, you often overresource to ensure everything goes well. The pilot group or division should be thoughtfully selected to increase the probability of a successful test. Best of all, this provides a proof of concept within your organization—a success that you can use to sell your internal team.

Pilots require the luxury of time. Based on the drivers for your sales force transformation, you may or may not have the time for a pilot. If you don't, the best alternative is to locate a comparable success from within your organization (if possible) or from a benchmark company in your industry. Sources for these types of stories include research organizations such as the Corporate Executive Board, Sirius Decisions, and Chief Sales Officer (CSO) Insights.

### Rollout to Frontline Managers First

First-level sales managers are among the most important people in realizing the success of your sales transformation effort. Whether it's sales training or better understanding the scope of a transformation effort, the front-line sales leaders should come first. After all, they're the ones who will help coach, model, and pass on the content and process to their teams. Ultimately, you need them to lead by example.

This sequence means that you must equip the sales managers and leaders to coach and reinforce from the start, which takes more than simply giving them the same content as the sales team. That's necessary, but not sufficient. Sales managers need to be trained on how to coach staff in the new sales strategy, processes, skills, and behaviors, and they also need to learn how to select, develop, and provide performance feedback to their teams based on the new processes. The Chally Group, an HR consulting and business analytics firm, has found that only 15 percent of top performing salespeople who are promoted to sales leadership roles ultimately succeed. In part that's because different skill sets and behaviors are required in that leadership role. Many sales managers were promoted into the role based on their success as salespeople, but they have never been trained or been given the proper tools to lead their sales team. It's a classic case of "what got you here won't get you there."

Your first-level sales leaders will help you maintain consistency throughout the organization and will help keep the team from lapsing into old behaviors and turning your transformation into nothing more than the flavor of the month. Ralph Chauvin, VP of sales at Perfetti Van Melle, a global confectioner, advised us on the importance of consistency. "Being inconsistent. That's what gets in the way," he said during our conversation about his sales transformation experience. "Managers going for flavor of the month." Ralph describes himself as ruthless in his consistency. "I constantly used and expected our managers and team to leverage our communications and sales approach, and that's all people heard from me. Extremely determined and focused and applied consistently. An inconsistent manager is the biggest barrier to any behavioral change."

Managers who are involved in the sales transformation from the beginning can also help you get more out of the "middle of the curve"—the 50 to 80 percent of the sales team that is neither at the very top nor the very bottom. As Lisa Redekop told us in an interview, "A great sales manager knows where your talent is, can motivate your sales talent, and knows it's not about the salespeople at the top 10 percent. It's

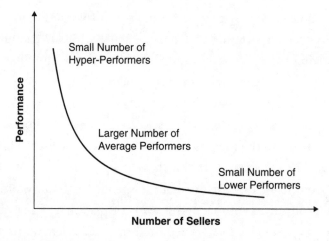

**Figure 7.1** Power Law Distribution.

about enabling the salespeople who are at the top 40 percent. If you can get more out of them you are getting more than if you motivate the top 10 percent." You will need your sales leaders to sustain and reinforce the change and, ultimately, to "move the middle." According to power law distributions (also known as the 80/20 rule) 50 percent or more of your sales can come from the hyperperformers who are at the beginning of the curve shown in figure 7.1; therefore, the objective is to move a few of your salespeople from average performers to top performers.

It's difficult to hire sales superstars or hyperperformers; you will need to hire others who can be developed and trained to be good, productive sellers, and these will likely make up the majority of your sales team. You'll need to rely on your first-level leaders to assess their teams and talent as a part of the transformation and determine who can truly support and excel in the future sales model.

### Avoid Death by a Thousand Cuts

Somewhat counterintuitively, in our research of successful sales transformations, we found that a majority of companies typically grew the size of their sales force, but still churned 20 to 50 percent of the sales team to update skills and capabilities. A healthy amount of turnover may be necessary to foster acceptance of a major transformation. Here's how Mike Dickerson, GM and EVP of Global Collaboration Services at PGi, described his experiences to us in an interview:

> You are transforming processes, a new way of doing things. Some of the people you have may not be suited to the work going forward. You have to shake some people out. It can create resentment or fear and anxiety among people you want to keep. If people are inspired by the vision and you get the folks to buy in, the ones who don't are the ones you need to get rid of anyway. But what's interesting, the ones in the middle, if they see that there's a legitimate place you are trying to go to, and they see the best performers who are their peers wanting to go to that place, and they see the laggards denigrating it and being resentful, the people in the middle don't rebel. Now you've inspired them. The stars and the folks in the middle rush toward the Promised Land! And you're moving aggressively toward changing out the people who need to be changed out.

Many sales leaders commented that it's best to make the team cuts at once, be transparent about the reasons, and communicate honestly and candidly. You want the remaining people to know that they're on the team and why. Avoid creating a culture of fear and uncertainty that can dramatically slow down the business while you're in the process of transforming. Lastly, not unlike the findings about mergers and acquisitions, value is maximized when there is early and timely execution of a few key fundamentals, such as the levers outlined in chapter 2 and the considerations outlined in this chapter. Despite all the apparent benefits of rapid execution, the "death by a thousand cuts" still damages many organizations.

In most companies there's going to be a group of employees who are on their way out. They've been with the organization too long, or they're disenfranchised one way or another. They are not going to be on the boat with you. Concentrate on identifying the change agents who *are* on board, who will evangelize transformation, and who will help carry that message to the entire team.

### *Keep It Simple*

Many of us have been guilty of mistaking complexity for competence. The more robust and thorough the account plan, the more details on a pipeline report, the more voluminous the sales playbook, the better. Or so we think. Tom Martin, a former president of sales training legend Miller-Heiman, and now an advisor to the sales effectiveness industry, told us in an interview that after working for seven different sales effectiveness firms, "I have seen many variations in approach to implementations—especially the tools used to support training. All of them had strengths and weaknesses in their models. [Miller-Heiman founder] Steve Heiman liked to position his tools, such as the one-page Blue Sheet®, as 'elegant in their simplicity.' We knew when competing against certain firms with 10- to 12-page plans that we needed to show the customer our completed Blue Sheet® and we encouraged them to ask the competing sellers to produce their opportunity plan. One point for our prospects was that if the person selling them wasn't using their tool, why should they? A second point was that even if they did have a completed plan it would take a lot longer to explain their 10 pages of notes than scanning an elegantly simple one-page form. With sales force transformations, it's KISS—Keep It Simple for the Sellers."

At the highest level of a company's strategy, the complexity issue is very real. In the massive study mentioned earlier in the chapter, the researchers found that middle managers, when asked about hurdles to understanding the company's strategy, were four times more likely to cite too many corporate priorities and strategic initiatives than to indicate a lack of clarity in communication. Many managers are confused as to what matters most, which is corroborated by the finding that only 55 percent of middle managers can name even one of their company's top five priorities. Simplicity does not mean simple; it's one of the hardest undertakings for the executive team to rigorously define, prioritize, and resource the vital few strategic imperatives that create a competitive advantage.

The key consideration from the standpoint of sales effectiveness is to build and deploy repeatable, easily understandable processes and tools, and this requires time and insightful consideration. Ultimately, if the sales force won't adopt or use the tool, it's not going provide value to the teams and drive results.

### *Measuring Progress: Sales Transformation Dashboard*

We've discussed metrics extensively throughout this book but have mainly focused on the initial and ongoing indicators. The sales transformation effort should have its own dashboard to measure progress and results—such as the number of solution-type deals, win ratios, wallet share, customer satisfaction or experience, among others—while also including interim metrics that show near-term progress and areas requiring course corrections. We've seen that when our clients don't routinely share progress and result metrics with the whole sales organization, the transformation effort loses momentum, excitement, and engagement. If you're watching a basketball game, and you didn't know the score or how much time is on the game clock, it's not as riveting as it would be if you knew the score was tied with one minute to go.

Lindsey Nelson echoed these thoughts in a conversation with us:

> You start to capture metrics, you look for trends and themes, and if they're strong enough they'll tell a story, and you can gain insight to take action on. I think we all agree if you are not measuring it, you can't manage it at all. We were amazed where we weren't measuring things. You get the question 'how am I doing?' Well, it feels good, but that won't get you far. Who can show me if it's working or isn't? You isolate the noise and the naysayers. Say you've introduced a new product into the mix. You've got a couple loud people complaining it's inhibiting their sales. They could be the exception, and everyone else is a success; they're just really loud, and we have to figure out what is unique to them that we can help with and quiet them down. The metrics and measurements go a long way to help you stand with clarity during change.

Larry Stack, global head of services sales for HP Enterprise, specifically focused on improvements in four key metrics as part of the company's sales transformation: number of new customers, overall win rate, percent of sales reps achieving quota, and sales costs. In a little over 18 months, Larry and his team were able to dramatically improve each of these key metrics via a renewed focus and ongoing reporting on those metrics. In a conversation, he described how these metrics also changed his philosophy on sales strategy. "I used to focus on capacity and now I focus on efficiency," he explained. In other words, he's found more success with fewer, highly effective sales professionals who are able to drive higher win rates and quota attainment than with just more "feet on the street."

As you track your progress with metrics, a key consideration is to focus on the essential few metrics that demonstrate that your sales transformation is working and is having the desired impact on your business and customers. Mike Conway, Carl Strenger, and many others told us that too often organizations produce metrics based on whatever data they can easily get their hands on. Unfortunately, this leads to too many metrics, some of which measure essentially the same thing, while few or none measure what really matters.

### Compensation and Incentives

Almost everyone associated with sales agrees that compensation is a key factor in driving the right behaviors and motivating the sales force. Most of the debate revolves around the degree to which compensation is a factor. Is it 50 percent of the equation? Or 80 percent? Numerous studies have supported our observation that things other than money are important to sellers. For example, a survey[4] conducted by the TAS Group asked sales reps what motivates them. While compensation accounted for 17 percent of responses, the thrill of the sale and recognition got 8 percent each, and making progress on a sale counted for the remaining 67 percent. This is not to say that compensation isn't important. In fact, below a certain threshold in salary, it may be more important. But for most reps making progress on a sale is the biggest motivator. Keeping that in mind, if making progress internally on an average deal requires a 20-page opportunity plan and daily meetings, then sellers are probably not going to be motivated, regardless of what you pay them. The frustrating, burdensome process will squelch any remaining motivation to sell. "Basically, salespeople do what you tell them to do," Steve Young told us. "You influence the sales team's behaviors through the comp program. You've got to change the comp program and the metrics."

As Steve suggests, there's a system for motivating a sales team. A 2013 Towers Watson research paper[5], "For Optimal Sales Force Performance, Pay Is Not Enough," explained that the most effective elements to strengthen the compensation program were built around a well-designed performance management program, effective sales managers, and frontline coaching and career development programs. This is supported by our own results in working with sales teams. If the sales force transformation is fundamentally aligned with a compelling driver and need for change, one of the outcomes should be to increase compensation for the sales team. Many salespeople want to be held accountable for their performance as long as they are given a fair chance at being successful. Sales leaders can hold them accountable by creating an environment conducive to success. This means providing absolute clarity in defining roles and priorities, providing the tools and training to follow through on those priorities, ensuring the measurements represent what good performance looks like, and aligning compensation and recognition with those measurements.

When your sales transformation is on track, you'll see it reflected in employee engagement surveys and in attrition levels. One sign that your team is unhappy with its compensation is your rate of voluntary attrition. Several companies reported that their attrition rate went from 20 to 25 percent before the sales transformation to 15 percent after.

### *Implementing Communications*

From a communications standpoint, "early and often" is a key principle. In sales, it's easy to get lost in the next deal or making the quarterly quota as opposed to paying attention to a long-term initiative that may take four to six quarters or longer to produce material changes. In executing your internal sales campaign, ongoing communication to the sales organization is critical to maintain top-of-mind awareness and momentum. Some key implementation considerations include the following:

- Create a communications plan and meeting cadence that includes weekly and monthly status reports based on a review of the sales transformation dashboard, which provides the metrics and insights to "manage up, out, and across" the organization.
- Schedule quarterly meetings with cross-functional stakeholders to re-review the overall initiative and to make adjustments as needed (e.g., increase scope, shift resources, change the sequence).
- Capture and communicate success stories along the way—even if only in simple 30-second video clips that highlight the desired change in behavior from your sales team or customers.

As Michael Conway told us in a conversation, "I see sales as a communication, a relationship. The most important person in communications is not the sender of the message, but the receiver of the message." In treating your sales force transformation like an internal sale, you need to determine the different communication vehicles you will use to determine what's most effective for each audience. For example, these vehicles might include email, newsletters, small group meetings, town hall meetings, or videos. As convenient as email may be, for instance, it might not the best way to communicate to sellers who are inundated with email and prioritizing communications from their customers over yours.

One of our clients would send a weekly update on its sales force transformation to everyone in the sales organization as well as to other key stakeholders throughout the company. The head of sales said that completing the weekly update was a "forcing factor" to get him to define and articulate the company's progress each week. Not unlike doing a status report for a project, completing the update helps crystallize one's thinking and determine progress (or lack thereof) since the previous update. There was another key feature of this communication: the head of sales kept it short and tight, which forced him to clarify his thinking and messages.

Lastly, when it comes to communications, the content's meaning is more important than its volume. Sending more emails or hosting more town hall meetings doesn't mean that your message will be better understood. In line with our "keep it simple" consideration, part of good communications is to be clear about what you want people to believe and remember. In general, if your communication contains more than three to five key messages, the sheer volume will dilute what's important.

### *Program Management*

Finally, there's a strong need to have a program management office or resources as part of the sales transformation team. The slog of implementation is all about status reports, work plans, and daily struggles to shift the status quo. There should be one team that focuses on the time, budget, and scope of the transformation initiative. We've found that this team needs to be headed by a strong leader who can quickly navigate the sales organization and escalate issues as required. You want someone who's an opinion leader in the sales organization—someone who can easily navigate the company's political landscape. Remember, you're putting too much time, money, and energy into the sales transformation to have a lower-level resource lead the day-to-day activities that will ultimately determine progress and results.

A program plan and core team will be needed to coordinate any external partners/resources who are hired to support the transformation. As any sales executive or airline mechanic will tell you, it's hard to fly a plane while you're changing the wings. In other words, you can't run a transformation in a timely fashion while still running the day-to-day business. In an interview with Mike Woodard, a sales enablement executive at GE, he talked with us about the importance of using a program plan to coordinate several external partners based on his experience of leading a sales transformation at PepsiCo earlier in his career: "The other piece is having great learning partners," he said. "In lockstep with me, throughout the process, going into the major transformation, I remember getting three different training companies on the phone. I said 'let's go around the horn and introduce ourselves.' I said 'you are not competitors; I need you to work together as one design team.'"

The head of the program office should have direct access to the chief sales officer (CSO) in case something needs to be escalated or accelerated, and he or she or she will need to support the transformation effort and facilitate the implementation slog. But the driver, sponsor, and key communicator should be the CSO. This is a role that cannot be outsourced.

And speaking of outsourcing, in chapter 8 we'll take a look at how to extend your sales force transformation to external parties—customers, suppliers, and partners—who can play a vital role in your efforts.

### Chapter 7: Key Considerations for Implementation—Takeaways

- Design and deploy the simplest, most useable tools possible.
- Whenever possible, try a pilot program with a small team before implementing transformation across the entire organization; it's like showing an external buyer a proof of concept.
- Always roll out a transformation initiative to frontline managers first; they're the ones who will model the right behaviors and manage to the new processes.
- Although a successful transformation will elevate your middle performers, you should always expect to have to reassign or cut some of the laggards.

- Measure progress in the near, mid, and long term—and share the results across the entire organization.
- Assign a dedicated leader to head up the transformation initiative; remember, you can't change an airplane's wings while you're in mid-flight.

# CHAPTER 8

# Extending Your Sales Transformation to Business Partners, Suppliers, and Customers

One of our clients asked us how to get more out of its ecosystem of business partners, suppliers, and customers. This client had been adding to that ecosystem of partners and suppliers almost indiscriminately—and many were a losing proposition. "We don't even know how many partners or suppliers we have," the senior director said, almost in embarrassment. "We also do not partner with our customers enough in creating next-generation products." The company thought that adding new partners should be focused on quantity as opposed to quality: more was better. As we researched the economics of the company's relationships, however, we found that adding more external relationships was just adding coordination and management costs; instead, the company needed to act more strategically. For example, this company was covering low-potential markets with high-cost business partners and was triple-sourcing suppliers when it made more sense to invest in one or two strategic ones. "We need to 80/20 our ecosystem and then invest in those that make economic and strategic sense," the senior director said when asked about what the company should do. Ultimately, the company pared the number of channel partners and suppliers by more than 50 percent and began to include customers in product ideation and development.

As more and more companies expand their ecosystems to improve coverage, just-in-time delivery and their overall solution sets, it becomes increasingly important for them to involve all of their external relationships in their sales transformation efforts. The entire ecosystem can benefit from a tighter coupling of the cocreation of value and the delivery of delightful customer experiences. Everyone wins.

## *Channel Partners*

Many companies refer to the channel as anything other than their direct sales forces. There are many different types of indirect channel partners. They're known as value-added resellers, distributors, fulfillment partners, manufacturers' reps or perhaps consulting partners. Regardless of what they're called, channel partners are stand-alone businesses that sell, distribute, or implement another company's offerings, and they receive some sort of compensation for their services.

For the purposes of sales transformation, your channel partners should be viewed as part of an overall go-to-market structure, namely, as another route to market. Other routes to market include the Internet as well as call centers, retail stores, and your direct sales force. The difference between these routes and channel partners is that you generally have no direct control over the latter. You can influence your channel partners through training, marketing development funds, deal registration processes, and other methods, but you ultimately have to use influence, not direct control. While you can "fire" a channel partner just as you would a direct seller, there may be some contractual constraints that you don't have where employees are concerned. One of the common challenges we see with fast growth sales teams is that they have not been selective enough in choosing channel partners. Similar to hiring a high-cost sales professional, you should have clear criteria for your selection process, and your due diligence should include site visits, reference checks, multiple interviews and discovery sessions, and more important, regular evaluations.

How do you gain influence with channel partners? It comes down to understanding their strategic objectives and initiatives and being able to give them information and suggestions that will help their businesses. This is not different from the internal sale we wrote about earlier, but this time the customers are your external partners. You must answer the "What's in it for them" question, just as you would with any key constituency. Collecting "voice of the partner" information is just as important as voice of the customer insights, which we've discussed in previous chapters. Current partners want to feel heard and understood. Whether you gather their feedback via surveys or in face-to-face discussions, it's important to capture their voice. For a number of our clients, conducting a joint planning session with each key channel partner was an invaluable activity. It helped each party align its measureable objectives, value propositions, and joint marketing and selling activities. Moreover, the joint planning session was a critical piece in establishing and growing trust, which may be the most important part of a channel partner relationship, similar to being a trusted advisor to key customers.

Along with the value proposition to your partners, you also need clear and unambiguous rules of engagement for working with them. These rules should encompass how you jointly sell, the partner's pricing and discount authority, the process of passing leads to each other, and the overall sales process insertion points. There will always be issue that must be resolved case by case, but clear rules of engagement are a best practice that will help guide the relationship. The rules of engagement will differ, however, based on your channel partner's approach and business model.

At this highest level, there are typically three approaches to channel partners:

- sell to
- sell through
- sell with

The first approach is where you could sell doors, for example, to a large retailer such as Home Depot or Lowe's, that then sell the doors to consumers through their retail stores and websites. The second approach is where you sell through a reseller, such as CDW, which sells various technology brands, among them HP and Microsoft, as part of a bundled solution. The third approach is where you sell with an alliance partner jointly and may even make sales calls together, for example, a software company might sell alongside a large system integrator like Accenture.

In each of the three approaches, the sales transformation vision needs to be shared with the channel partner because the partner directly impacts the sales process and performance. If you want to realize all your go-to-market synergies, then including your channel partners as part of your sales transformation effort is not optional.

Another key driver of utilizing channel representation is market coverage. Being able to quickly cover a fast growing market with established partners that are already in a territory can be a significant value-add for your company. The time-to-market advantage is important, as is the ability to leverage existing partner relationships to sell through. This is especially true in foreign or emerging markets, where leveraging existing businesses means a lower up-front investments and less financial risk.

One telecommunications company was struggling several years ago to cover its full market opportunity. "I don't think we need to hire a bunch of salespeople for territories that just don't yield a lot," the vice president of sales told us. We were talking about his channel strategy and how he could use manufacturer reps and implementation partners to better cover territories that didn't have enough opportunity for a permanent employee. The company was keeping its eyes on the sales budget; the cost of sales had been increasing, and the division's president was looking for ways to lower it. "We need to use the account managers for our most strategic accounts and the channel for everything else," he said when asked about a go-to-market structure. The channel was thought to be less costly because the manufacturer reps worked on pure commission, and the implementation partners were willing to take less margin, such as a partner discount, if they could secure the implementation work.

The vice president of sales began to shift his bestsellers to high-growth markets and accounts and left the territories with lower potential to channel partners. The execution of this strategy can be challenging as you often need channel managers to work with the partners, but the act of transforming the sales organization can be significant— new routes to market, new strategic sellers, and a new focus on market potential and opportunity. We have seen numerous clients begin to change how they cover their "pyramid of clients," which, as you can see in figure 8.1, puts the largest, most strategic customers at the top, the midmarket ones in the middle and the smallest at the bottom. Many companies have begun to use more channel partners at the bottom and middle of the pyramid while focusing their most expensive, direct sales resources on their strategic accounts.

What this means is that channel partners may "touch" more of your customers, which is why it's essential for them to be part of the transformation. They're going to have to sell the message to the market and to customers. Besides, some of the small and medium-sized customers will become strategic accounts, and it's important for them to have the right buying experience from the beginning.

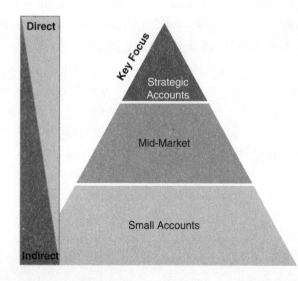

**Figure 8.1** Pyramid of Clients.

When companies share too little information with their channel partners out of a fear that this information will wind up in the hands of the competition, they risk falling short in extending the sales force transformations to those partners. Executive teams typically do not have consensus on how much information to share. The default answer often is "This is proprietary information!" And subsequently, the teams don't share anything. But sharing too little is a bigger risk than sharing too much, especially when you think about the investment you've made in your sales transformation. In addition, if the channel is primarily serving the customers and the sellers in the channel have a different message than your direct sellers, the customers can be confused by mixed messages. Part of building trust and driving value with a partner is sharing information and insights and presenting a common message to the market.

Some Actions You Can Take with Channel Partners Include the Following:

- *Bring them into the transformation process early on.* At a minimum, include your channel partners in a kickoff call and ask for their feedback on what's most important to them and what they are hearing from their customers. You want to create a joint value proposition with your channel partners. It should include building trust and sharing plans and strategies as you launch your transformation. Typically, a channel manager could be responsible for a few large partners or a portfolio of partners and this manager should help to involve the partners early on in the process by coaching and leading them regarding pipeline reviews, deal support, and optimizing the customer experience.
- *Create a one-page value proposition document for each channel partner group.* For example, you may have consulting or fulfillment partners or use value-added resellers. You must answer the "What's in it for them" for each partner group to build excitement for and engagement with the transformation while providing the partners with materials to help them pass on the message internally.

- *Use a technology platform to share relevant information with the different partner tiers.* Many technology companies have created robust channel partner programs that tier channel partners by size and strategic value. This helps a company calibrate the investments it makes in its partners through training, marketing, and shared resources, among others. Information and data can be shared via access to online portals, customer or partner relationship management tools, and company resources. Companies such as Salesforce.com and Workday use these tools to influence and communicate to different tiers of channel partners.
- *Leverage Marketing Development Funds (MDF) to align a partner's sales approach with your own.* Companies as diverse as IBM, Microsoft, Herman Miller, and Steelcase have used this pool of money to fund a rollout of their new sales process and methodologies (in IBM's case, for example, its custom-built "Signature Selling Method") to their channel partners to align the entire ecosystem on a consistent sales and service approach.
- *Continuously evaluate your channel partners' performance.* If they aren't adding value and are not on board with your sales strategy, you shouldn't invest time or effort in them. Just as you don't want too many products and services, it's important to rationalize your channel partner ecosystem and invest in those channel partners who share your excitement and align with your transformational vision. Partners who aren't adding expertise regarding your products or services or who are not fully leveraging marketing development funds may not be good candidates for investment in the form of training, discounts, or resource support.

## Suppliers

We see this happening time after time: A seller promises delivery of a certain product by a specific date but then can't deliver on the promise because of supply chain issues or disruptions. With many parts and products manufactured overseas, the delivery time can be material and challenges may be hard to fix quickly. If your sales transformation enables you to sell more products, that should help your suppliers. After all, the holy grail of many businesses is tightly aligning customer demand with supply chains so you can better manage inventory while having full visibility and transparency of the customer lifecycle from initial contact to cash payment.

Just as you embarked on your sales force transformation with voices of the customer and partner, you should similarly conduct a "voice of the supplier" discovery effort to determine ways in which the supply chain will be impacted by your sales force transformation. This is also a great time to confirm what the supply chain may need from your sales team—items such as forecasts, market trends, and end-user insights. On this last point: Suppliers often want to know how their products and parts are being received in the marketplace. Sharing frontline insights with your suppliers is a great way to build trust and help them be more successful.

Many companies have implemented some sort of CRM system, which helps them to effectively manage leads, contacts, accounts, and opportunities. Fewer companies have implemented a supplier relationship management (SRM) system, which helps develop mutually valuable relationships with strategic suppliers to deliver greater levels of competitive advantage than would be possible through a typical transactional relationship. The SRM model is not about a system per se but about helping to keep a close and fruitful relationship with your strategic suppliers. For many firms, if you can't deliver or ship a product, you can't recognize the revenue, which can negatively impact the stock price and senior executives' compensation.

The date on which one of our clients shipped its product was always a critical area for executives because that was the point at which they could recognize the revenue. The "book ship" date was a key field in their CRM system and was discussed on most pipeline calls, especially in the last few weeks of a quarter. Make no mistake: supply chain delays and disruptions are serious issues that directly impact sales and the customer experience. For some companies, especially in the manufacturing sector, a sales transformation that doesn't include strategic suppliers is destined to fail.

We worked with one company that had a lot of discord with one of its suppliers. The supplier thought the company was always trying to nickel-and-dime it. We interviewed the supplier, which saw our client as a tyrant. As part of our implementation of a new sales process, we assembled a small team comprised of stakeholders from each company—the supplier and our client. As part of the initial conversations, our client talked about how it wanted to sell more solutions with a value proposition focused on high quality and speed to market. Although our client dual-sourced many of its supplies, it was willing to single-source if a supplier could demonstrate that it was reliable and had a plan focused on quality. The supplier began to see an opportunity with our client and was willing to invest some time to develop a more strategic and deeper relationship. During our meetings it became clear that our client's value proposition was dependent on having its suppliers buy into its transformation. Our client could save money and increase productivity with more strategic relationships with key suppliers that were reliable, consistent, and quality-focused. After all, double or triple sourcing requires coordination and has opportunity costs. "Why not invest more [time, money, and effort] into a few suppliers vs. keeping score based on pennies and aggravation?" one of our client stakeholders remarked to us after a meeting. Within six months, our client began to single-source with the supplier and the relationship was more cordial, with a regular cadence of meetings each quarter to ensure things stayed on track.

In order to marry up the demand and supply chains, you must ensure that the demand chain stakeholders (sales/marketing) are talking to the supply chain stakeholders. If there is better insight into customer demand, the supply chain can make sure it's ready to produce and ship what's in demand. Developing close relationships with suppliers is like growing customer relationships where you often want to grow margins while deepening the relationship. In the book *Powered by Honda: Developing Excellence in the Global Enterprise*, the authors cite a key reason why Honda typically has higher profit margins than Toyota: "[It] is the inclusive relationships with their strategic suppliers, in which these suppliers are literally considered extensions of Honda."[1]

Other companies such as Walmart, Cisco, General Electric, and Dell have refined their supply chains to serve as a competitive advantage for their businesses. Increasingly, companies like these are using smart supply chains powered by technology to communicate in real time. One example is Taleris, a joint venture between Accenture and GE Aviation that leverages a digital network of sensors and analytics to predict potential aircraft maintenance faults while recommending preventative actions. The goal is to "predict, prevent and recover from operational disruptions—improving operational efficiency and enhancing the customer experience"[2]—something many organizations share.

Like partners, suppliers need to be part of the early conversations around a transformation and have a seat at the table to discuss their perspectives. Top-notch suppliers that focus on world-class quality and delivery are rare and need to be treated like a strategic partner or customer. When sales executives miss their numbers or upset a customer because they can't deliver a product when they've promised, they often realize how important suppliers are to their success.

With the SRM model in mind, here are some actions you can take with suppliers:

- *Create a supplier advisory board.* Its role is to help bring together all strategic suppliers to share the company's strategy and solicit feedback and suggestions from key suppliers. The board might meet once a quarter via conference call and annually in a face-to-face summit, which could include some joint training and collaborative business planning.
- *Start a supplier program office and/or appoint a supplier "account manager" to help manage relationships and keep strategies and initiatives aligned.* The account manager would conduct monthly or quarterly business reviews with each top supplier to review progress on joint initiatives, operational performance, and supply chain risks.

- *Use a Supplier, Input, Process, Output, and Customer) (SIPOC) diagram to better understand the path and process from supplier to customer.* Share the diagram with your suppliers and see what they would add. Similar to a "buyer's journey" map, which you often create as part of developing a buyer-aligned sales process, the SIPOC diagram depicts the "product journey" from supplier to customer.
- *Leverage technology to connect and communicate among your customers, sales force, and supply chain.* Identify areas to leverage technology from automating sales forecasts to embedding sensors in your products that will increase the amount of communication and insight throughout your supply chain.

### *Customers*

In our survey we asked about the degree of customer involvement in sales transformations. More than half the respondents said their customers had little or no involvement in their transformation. Yet, all the sales executives who've experienced successful sales organization transformations told us that customers were aligned with the initiative. The best three-predictor model, which explains about 57 percent of the variance in whether the sales transformation is rated a success, includes the variables of (1) involving customers; (2) gaining buy-in; and (3) measuring progress. The customer variable highlights the importance of the outside-in perspective and of cocreating and collaborating with your customers.

Many books have been written and consulting projects focused on enhancing the customer's experience. This experience is shaped by numerous factors including advertising, referrals, the buying process, prior experience with a product or service, and third-party reviews. In enterprise business-to-business markets, your sales force is instrumental in shaping the customer's initial impression of your brand. Numerous studies have shown that the sales force is key to building and maintaining a strong business-to-business brand. It has been shown that the most important driver of brand equity is the salesperson's behavior, followed by his or her personality, product quality, and nonpersonal marketing communications.[3] While your customers can provide only limited input into your future innovation efforts, they can offer a wealth of knowledge on how to improve your sales and service, especially if they have their direct knowledge of your competition.

As Central Garden & Pet's Paul Duval told us about his company's journey through a sales transformation, "When you come out of this, you get that there is no one-size-fits-all solution. You have to look at your sales force with what I'll call an efficiency index to your ROI. [In our transformation] we learned how much torque we'd need to deliver to the customer. The selling effort per dollar of revenue isn't always the same. The customers are different, the channels are very different, and sometimes the selling process is different." In other words, you need a flexible strategy for making key customers part of your transformation.

One advantage of involving your customers is that they can help you sell to them and cocreate the very products and services they want to buy. The cocreation approach has value because customers know better than you what it's like and what it should be like to be your customer.

Microsoft has used cocreation to create award-winning ad formats. The company has worked with consumers to cocreate online ads that are more engaging and provide better value. Microsoft asked various constituency groups what role different technologies have in their lives, how brands can earn their loyalty, and what role technology plays in their purchase decisions. As an extension to any voice of the customer work, the cocreation concept takes the process one step further—working side by side with your customers to create products they want to buy and to improve their experience. From a sales standpoint, if customers are involved in cocreating a product, they are more likely to buy it.

In another example concerning cocreation crowdsourcing, software giant SAP manages a website called "Idea Place" to engage its global customer base to submit new product ideas and participate in contests and other innovation campaigns. Product managers from across SAP can set up an "idea session" for their products to capture customer feedback and ideas. The customer will often be involved in the entire product life cycle, including product launch and beyond. After two years, Idea Place had more than 600 crowdsourced ideas implemented or in development for release in SAP products.

Another area where we've found it particularly beneficial to include customers is account planning. Many of our clients have created account plans—some good, some bad—for their largest accounts. We had one client that had more than 20 people on one account, which bought over $100 million of their products and services every year. In many respects, the account was a midsized business in its own right. In the account planning process, it's important create the plan with an outside-in perspective and to validate it with the customer. From the standpoint of change management, asking customers for input and incorporating input into the plan is key to including them and will help create deeper engagement with customers as well. As part of an overall account management excellence program and cadence, the plan should be reviewed internally each quarter and should also be revalidated with the customer. As you'll see from the actions we're about to recommend, many customers want to be listened to and have their input or recommendations acted upon or at least have them acknowledged and followed up on.

Some actions you can take with customers include the following:

- *Create a customer advisory board.* Similar to the supplier board, the customers might meet once a quarter via conference call and annually in a face-to-face summit, which could include some breakout sessions on cocreation and could capture feedback on new products and initiatives. We've helped set up a number of customer advisory boards, and although there is some risk (e.g., a customer criticizes a product or experience), we've never had a client regret setting one up. The benefits far outweigh the risks.

- *Pilot a process of cocreating something with one of your key customers.* It might start with something as simple as an online ad that can then evolve to touch on new product development and strategic initiatives. The cocreation test or pilot can emanate from the customer advisory board based on which customers would be most interested and engaged in the process.

- *Shadow a customer as part of the buyer's journey.* This may help align your sales process with the customer's buying process, which—as we've pointed out—may be part of a sales transformation. If you can't shadow your customer, you can at least interview the key buyer(s) to understand the process they went through to purchase your product and to understand where value is created or destroyed along the path. Sales transformations need to put the customer first. As Peter Drucker once wrote, "The purpose of business is to create and keep a customer."[4]

## Your Partners and Customers Want You to Be Successful

The bottom line on channel partners, suppliers, and customers: keep them out of your transformation initiative at your own peril; their strategic involvement increases your chance of success. The degree of their inclusion in your sales transformation effort will depend on your business and go-to-market model, but each constituency should be thought about and considered as you craft your vision and gain buy-in both internally and externally. Many of our clients are creating customer advisory boards and reviewing their channel strategies as they search for new ways to grow the top line and create innovative, cutting-edge products. One of the key principles in sales is to listen more than you talk. The same principle applies to your partners and suppliers. Ask them good questions and listen to them carefully. They want to help you to be successful.

Next up, we'll cover how to sustain your transformation as an ongoing initiative once it's launched.

*Chapter Eight: Extending Your Sales Transformation to Business Partners, Suppliers, and Customers—Takeaways*

- As more companies expand their channels to improve coverage and speed up time to market, they must involve these channels in their sales transformation.
- Gain influence with channel partners by first understanding their strategic objectives and giving them information and suggestions that will help their businesses.
- In addition to CRM systems, companies need Supplier Relationship Management (SRM) systems to help manage the supplier relationship and improve the marriage of supply chain and demand chain for stronger sales and increased efficiency.
- More than half the respondents to our sales force transformation survey said their customers had little or no involvement in their transformation, but every successful transformation we know of involved customers as well as suppliers, channel partners, and internal resources.
- We recommend forming advisory boards comprising partners, suppliers, and customers.

# CHAPTER 9

# Sustaining Your Sales Transformation

Although this is our final chapter covering the sales transformation approach, and the final step (step 7) in our sales transformation process, it may be the most important. As you can guess, there's little value in investing time, money, and effort in transforming a sales organization only to see it then revert back to the earlier status quo. The ability to sustain your gains and improvements is critical to realizing a significant return on your investment in transformation.

There are a number of parallels in terms of physical transformation:

- According to Wellsphere, a website sponsored by Stanford University, only 5 percent of people who lose weight on a crash diet will keep the weight off.[1]
- A study published in April of 2013 in the *Journal of the American Medical Association* showed that one in four men did not make a single lifestyle change after a heart attack, stroke, or other major cardiac event.[2]
- According to *Men's Health* magazine, more than 91 percent of people who start an exercise regimen abandon it before the habit has taken hold.[3]

The message is clear: Unless you invest significant effort to reinforce and sustain your transformation gains, whether personal or professional, you are likely to revert to the previous status quo. We have seen this happen to numerous sales training and transformation projects:

- A high-technology firm invested almost $1 million to upgrade its sales organization with a new solution selling process, software sales specialists, CRM technology, and updated solution playbooks. After an initial surge, the effort lost momentum as indicated by lower customer satisfaction scores, deteriorating pipeline metrics, and decreased sales activity. Less than nine months after implementation, both the head of sales and the CEO were replaced when revenues continued to decline.

- An engineering services firm invested in a new sales process and selling skills programs to complement its deep expertise in design, building, and project management services. After training all cross-functional team members, sales, and engineering, one of the sales leaders established a cadence to talk about key clients and opportunities. The same sales leader was also tasked with keeping the training program alive through ongoing coaching and development. It quickly became clear that this sales leader was not fully engaged in coaching the sales team and lacked the ability to sustain change. The sales team was small and set in its ways. With little to no coaching, it soon returned to its previous state. Within one year the sales leader was reassigned to a sales role, and many of the sales team members were dismissed. The program was halted. What no one had considered was that the amount of energy required to launch the program was the same amount needed to drive change. Ultimately, the sales leadership, many sales team members, and the CEO were terminated.

- A Fortune 500 hardware and software company tried to be more of a solutions provider by offering a combination of product, services, and intellectual property. The company's gross margins had been decreasing as a result of selling more undifferentiated hardware that had a lower margin. All of the salespeople were trained on selling solutions and managing opportunities better. Ultimately, the changes were not sustained as there was too much leadership turnover, and the underlying processes were still built on siloed products and an engineering culture, including an 80-page PowerPoint deck explaining how to create a quote for a customer. This sort of overkill had a chilling effect on the sales process and the customer experience.

Sustaining a sales force transformation requires ongoing development, measurement, communications, and a management cadence— themes that have been interwoven throughout this book. We'll touch on these next, while also including specific actions you can take in each area to improve your ability to sustain the transformation.

## *Ongoing Development*

One way to tell that a sales transformation has taken place is when you can see new skills and behaviors on the part of managers and sellers. Many sales force transformations have emphasized a new or different customer conversation and the ability of the sales team to bring insights to customers as part of the sales process—sometimes with the objective of transcending the value of the product or service being offered. Sustaining these new skills and behaviors requires ongoing development and reinforcement. We don't recommend three- or four-day classes in windowless conference rooms, but on-demand or just-in-time (JIT) learning modules, lunch-and-learns, and best-practices sharing. Also, a sales training program is a key piece to inculcate the new skills and behaviors right from the start. Let's touch on JIT learning and training as two areas to concentrate on up-front for sustaining your sales transformation.

JIT was originally developed as an inventory strategy that companies used to increase efficiency and decrease waste by receiving supplies only as they were needed in the production process. Numerous studies have shown that we learn best when the training involves small "chunks" of content that we can apply immediately.

In sales, there's a higher adoption and absorption of new skills when role-playing is used in the training and when people are given an immediate opportunity to apply what they have learned. Compared to a "learning by listening" approach, this process can increase retention from 10 percent to more than 65 percent after three months.[4] In terms of a sales transformation, we've seen the JIT learning approach manifested in a number of ways, such as the following:

- Creating short videos (one to five minutes) that reinforce selling skills, such as qualifying, discovering, and negotiating, and that can be watched on a phone or tablet.
- Developing checklists or one-page tools that sellers can carry with them to review before sales calls or meetings.
- Assembling industry or role primers for sellers who are calling on diverse industries and contacts—with a lookup feature on a portal to find the industry or role (for example, for reviewing what matters most to a CFO before calling on anyone in that role).
- Equipping first-level sales managers to incorporate development into regular sales meetings with "meetings-in-a-box" covering selling skills or methods (such as pipeline management, opportunity/ deal qualification, or solution positioning).

Ongoing development reinforces a message to the sales organization: *This is the knowledge and these are the skills and abilities that are important to know and use, that will lead to increased and more consistent success, and that will also be measured and monitored.* This message is especially important when you hire and train new sales employees. Ongoing development also demonstrates your commitment to sustaining your sales force transformation to all of your internal stakeholders. They need to know that their input and efforts were not part of a one-time event.

During the training process, new employees gain the necessary knowledge and skills to become fully productive as soon as possible; this is a critical component of your organization's ongoing development. In both our research and our survey, we found successful sales transformations are more likely to increase the number of sales professionals employed by the organization. You need to inculcate them with your new way of sales. For new sellers, an effective training experience is particularly important because accelerating the time to full productivity has significant economic ramifications for a company. Like ongoing development, training also clearly signals to new employees what's important to the sales organization. An effective training program sustains the transformation by aligning desired skills and behaviors with the desired future state.

A final component of ongoing development is to keep a pulse on what's changing in your ecosystem. Nothing stands still: your customers, competitors, partners, and suppliers are all constantly changing. In 2001, Jim Collins authored one of the bestselling business books of all time: *Good to Great*.[5] In this classic work, Jim and his team examined 1,435 companies and arrived at 11 that had made a transition from "good" to "great"— in some cases, through a significant overall business transformation. Fourteen years later, where are those companies? Of the original 11, only 2 have outperformed the market, which led to another book by Collins: *How the Mighty Fall*.[6] The lessons from these companies help to inform what we know about sustaining a sales force transformation. The need to change and improve is ongoing, and in some cases a massive change is needed. This realization reminds us of the old African parable: "Every morning in Africa, a gazelle wakes up, it knows it must outrun the fastest lion, or it will be killed. Every morning in Africa, a lion wakes up. It knows it must run faster than the slowest gazelle, or it will starve. It doesn't matter whether you're the lion or a gazelle—when the sun comes up, you'd better be running."[7]

The following is a list of action steps for ongoing development:

- Assess the current sales training assets and tools that you have and determine what can be chunked into small bites for easy consumption, through multiple devices, by the sales force.
- Ensure that all sales employees have a Personal Development Plan (PDP). If they do not, create a simple one-page PDP for employees

to review individually with their managers on a quarterly basis to ensure they are stakeholders in their own ongoing development.

- Review each training component and make sure it aligns with the desired future skills and behaviors that are part of the sales transformation. For example, if the training program mainly consists of siloed product training when you're trying to sell holistic solutions, you'll need to reorient the program to better reflect the sales strategy.

### *Measurement*

We've touched on the topic of measurement throughout this book because (a) it's central to the sales organization, and (b) sellers generally "get it." If the numbers are improving—or if they're not improving, and you don't know why—measurement can show progress and provide insight; it can help you make intelligent decisions about what to do next. To sustain gains of your sales transformation, the key pieces should include a monthly dashboard on progress/results that's shared throughout the company, in addition to monthly Plus/Delta exercises focusing on what's working well (plus) and what should be changed (delta) to sustain the improvements achieved. A simple dashboard with a couple of key elements is shown in figure 9.1. A typical dashboard might have eight to ten key metrics or performance indicators. The challenge is to show ten or fewer. Too many metrics can dilute the focus and confuse priorities.

Transformation results should always be tied to corporate results. That means showing the alignment with the overall strategy, such as growing revenues, expanding gross margins, or improving the customer experience. We recommend conducting a win/loss analysis to better understand what is and is not working out in the field with live opportunities. Capturing voice of the customer (VOC) insights is critical to measuring and tracking what drives value for the entire organization.

In addition to these metrics, you'll need a set of measures on the desired behaviors of your sales transformation. After all, the blood,

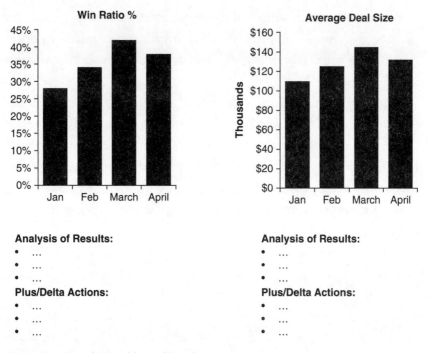

**Figure 9.1** Sample Monthly Dashboard.

sweat, and tears you have invested in your sales transformation have ultimately gone toward changing the conversation between your sales team and your customers. How is this working? How do you track the leading indicators that will predict whether you achieve your financial results? Mo Bunnell, founder of Bunnell Idea Group, developed a personal habit that he's included as part of his training programs to transform sales teams, especially where the relationship with the customer is paramount to the sale.

For a long time, Mo carried around an 1899 silver dollar that had once belonged to his grandfather. If you'd seen Mo's daily ritual of clutching the coin in his palm every morning and then slipping it into his pocket, you might have guessed he was superstitious or that he had a touch of obsessive-compulsive disorder. Hardly. Mo's daily silver dollar ritual was a deliberate act that helped him focus and set priorities for each day, making him the successful sales consultant and entrepreneur he is today. As Mo told us, "In the mornings I used to pick that coin up and think of the most proactive thing I could do that day," he says. "Then, I didn't allow myself to put it in my pocket until I knew what that thing was—and I couldn't take it out again until I'd done it."

That's not superstition; it's discipline. Mo continued this practice until he no longer needed the silver dollar to remind him. Today, when Mo is working with business development teams, he ensures that their frontline managers are in the trenches with their teams, shaping those behaviors into the right ones. "You do that by sharing data, sharing leading indicators, using give-to-gets, doing the weekly planning, using lead generation techniques."

As Jim Barksdale, the former CEO of Netscape, once said, "The main thing is to make the main thing, the main thing."[8] The basis of continuous improvement is to have consistent measurement checkpoints and to rapidly learn from plan-do-check-act cycles to keep the transformation momentum going and make needed corrections along the way.

A list of action steps for measurement follows:

- Maintain the metrics dashboard that was used during the transformation to help sustain the gains and include a component that provides causes and actions if metrics slip from targets or previous levels.
- Develop a win/loss program that, at a minimum, reviews a subset of deals on a monthly basis to learn whether new messaging, skills, and behaviors are resonating with prospects and customers. The basis of the win/loss review should be on development and lessons learned rather than on blame and fault-finding. The foundational question is, "What will we do differently next time?"
- Create (or extend if this was created as a part of your original gap assessment) an ongoing VOC program that measures customer satisfaction and engagement to determine what's "sticking" with customers; this extends the effort and process that was launched during the up-front assessment. We've found that the key here is to ensure you make the feedback actionable and then follow up with

customers. What are you doing and how is it working? If you're not going to be transparent and accountable for taking action on customer feedback, don't do it. It could hurt more than help.

## *Communications*

Attention scarcity is a major issue today—and it's only going to get worse. There's so much information and so many applications vying for our attention. For sales professionals it's an enormous challenge to satisfy external customers while also paying attention to internal initiatives and projects, such as transformation. But as we discussed earlier when it comes to change, a seller's allegiance is usually to what pays the bills— building customer relationships and meeting quotas. Everything else takes a backseat, including a sales transformation. As such, communications become critical to staying top of mind with the sales organization. From the standpoint of sustainment of your transformation, this means using tools and techniques, such as newsletters (keep them short and to the point) and dashboards, that show the results you're achieving and success stories that describe what's working for your colleagues.

Similar to an annual "value review" that you may do with a customer, you need to do the same with the sales organization to sustain your transformation gains and build momentum for additional improvement efforts. Communications to the sales organization should be treated like external communications, that is, ongoing, creative, and targeted. It's basically internal marketing, which is why some organizations brand their sales transformation in a way that's memorable and compelling.

Your sales organization will want to hear from leadership early and often, both during the sales transformation and afterward. This requires sales and company leaders to be "present" through town hall meetings, small group meetings, and one-on-one interactions. We've seen several sales leaders leverage online blogs to communicate the current state, share wins and metrics, and also highlight areas that need improvement. One of the levers we identified was leadership, and the ability of sales leaders to demonstrate ongoing commitment is a key factor that distinguishes a sustainable transformation from a one-time training event.

A recent example of senior leader communications comes from the auction house Sotheby's. Sotheby's was founded in 1744 and is currently the oldest company listed on the New York Stock Exchange; it has a long history of intense competition with its main global competitor, Christie's. At the beginning of 2015, both companies sought new leadership. At Sotheby's, Tad Smith was named CEO with a mandate to pursue profitable growth. While the company has realized record revenues on the strength of the global market for contemporary and modern art (one example is the 2014 sale of Alberto Giacometti's *Chariot* for $101 million to hedge fund billionaire Stephen Cohen), Sotheby's has struggled with profitability due to intense competition. In addition, the company's profitability was constrained by offering sellers a guarantee of a minimum amount, a policy that transferred a large amount of financial risk to the auction house. In the case of the Giacometti sale, this guarantee was estimated at $103 million, which resulted in a loss for Sotheby's of $2 million or more depending on marketing costs.[9] Tad has been working quickly to drive an overall cultural change at Sotheby's, and as he has stated publicly, "We will not roll dice in the auction room with shareholders' money."[10] He is personally setting an example for the sales organization (and investors) regarding the changes he is leading in the company and the sales organization specifically.

To enable communications across global organizations, there are some compelling technologies that enable ongoing communications as well as JIT learning, such as Chatter by Salesforce.com and Yammer. Many companies are using these tools to enable "organic," field-driven communications. One of our spouses works for Workday, a cloud computing company focused on enterprise software—the technology that runs big business in areas such as human resources, payroll, and finance. Workday has implemented Chatter to enable the sales teams to communicate in real time with headquarters and with one another. For example, a salesperson may post a last-minute question to the company, and her peers will provide answers supported by relevant content: a case study, a sales presentation, or links to a demo. For Workday and other companies that have fully adopted these collaboration tools, they offer a way to provide their sales teams with JIT information and reinforce that their sales teams and the company as a whole form a community.

A list of action steps for communications follows:

- Develop a weekly newsletter about the transformation. Keep it to one page and include, at a minimum, some measurement pieces, a success story, and the next milestone. You can also include a weekly prize for the best success story.
- Develop a communications pack for managers to use during team or one-on-one meetings with their direct reports. The pack can include FAQs, conversation prompts, or insights to share about the transformation. The managers are key assets to use in passing on the transformation messages to the sales teams, and the first-line sales manager is often the most important.
- As with an external marketing campaign, track internal communications and campaign components to see how you might change the mix to better inform and engage the sales organization. As in the VOC work, you also want to capture some voice of business feedback (such as a sales community you can tap to take the pulse of the organization) to ensure that you can better calibrate your messages and communications going forward.
- Implement a tool (such as Chatter or Yammer) that will enable collaboration throughout your sales team—the most powerful reinforcement often comes from peers.

### Management Cadence

We've written about the power of creating an ongoing sales management cadence to gauge how performance measures up to the plan, to coach and develop a team, and to anticipate and mitigate future issues and challenges. A cadence is a process of scheduling one-on-

one and team sales meetings and reviews on a weekly, monthly, and quarterly basis.

We've seen numerous transformations revert back to the previous status quo when the sales leader did not own and pass on a strong management cadence. Overall, it's not unlike managing a complex deal with a long sales cycle. A sales manager would not just check in with the sales team on day one and again six months later to ensure the deal was closed. The sales manager would test and review the progress, risks, and status of the deal throughout the sales cycle. The meetings could be once a week or every other week, and then a more thorough review could occur after any major event. The sustainment of the transformation should be treated the same way—that is, it is an ongoing process of reviewing progress and strategizing on how to close any gaps between goals and performance and better leverage successes.

If the transformation concerns becoming a solution-oriented sales organization, then the cadence conversations should be concerned with developing holistic solutions, average deal sizes, and team selling. In this case, if the conversations are more oriented to the number of calls or volume, then they're not aligned with the transformation objectives and should be changed.

In addition to the first-line sales manager conducting this cadence, the second- and third-level sales leaders need to ensure they're passing on the same message and processes—right up to the chief sales officer (CSO). As numerous CSOs have told us, they need to be careful about what they say and do; often they are taken either too literally or completely out of context, and this can create a downstream scramble around priorities. The CSO and sales leaders should also have a standard cadence and schedule to review similar areas as their first-level sales managers; however, the former are usually concerned with the organization's top accounts and opportunities rather than with routine pipeline management. The lesson here? What the CSO and sales leaders pay attention to and ask about speaks volumes about the sales organization and what's important. The transformation must be sustained via a cascade from the top. Start by having your sales managers schedule at least a monthly meeting with each of their direct reports to review each seller's performance, top accounts/opportunities, and some lessons learned in the last month as well as what each has planned for the next month. Be sure to develop standard agendas for the cadence meetings and share these with the sales teams; there should be no surprises regarding what will be covered in these meetings. Stick to development, learning, and improving performance.

Sales leaders need to stay on top of these meetings. They'll be seen as much more powerful when actions are tracked and reviewees are held accountable for follow-up and follow-through. Therefore, create a simple way to track cadence meeting outcomes and actions. Many sales leaders create management-only fields in a CRM or have the sales manager track each seller in a separate document.

Another good tactic to drive cadence: conduct field reviews or ride-alongs at least quarterly with each member of the sales team to improve development in sales calls and meetings and to see how the new skills and behaviors are being applied in the field. For the sales manager, ride-alongs are also a great way to capture VOC. There's a wealth of information to observe during a sales call. If the sales transformation changes are not being seen and heard during a sales call, then consider making changes in communications, training, and coaching to ensure the new skills and behaviors are filtering down to street level.

A final component of your management cadence should involve keeping a pulse on your team. As Jim Champy, celebrated consultant and author of numerous books including *Reengineering the Corporation: A Manifesto for Business Revolution*,[11] told us in an interview, "Since the last bubble in 2000, there's been a real failure to think about sustainability," about developing people in their organizations and understanding what they want and need over time. This requires empathy, says Jim. "You have to really understand what the people you are trying to advise are going through." Everyone has a story to tell. Knowing how to listen is critical. "Always realize how much you don't know," says the humble 70-year-old bestselling author. "Every day, I'm struck by how much I'm still learning." The best sales leaders, the ones who are able to sustain and reinforce change, are usually the best listeners.

A list of action steps for sales management cadence follows:

- Lay a foundation for cadence comprising a review of previous efforts and a next-step action plan.
- Use effective coaching and questioning to develop strategies and actions that help to solve a customer's issue, deliver measureable value, and close the performance gap.
- Put good data integrity and governance in place to ensure effective decisions and update all front-office tools and applications.
- Rationalize meetings as much as possible: people can't be in meetings all the time, and they may shut down unless the meetings offer a good return on effort invested.
- Ensure the cadence reviews are helping to drive the business: brainstorm solutions, strategize, provide support, and knock down barriers!

Throughout this book we've discussed numerous ways to build the ability to reinforce and sustain your sales transformation efforts, such as executive sponsorship, alignment with other functions, and including key stakeholders as part of the transformation design.

At Central Garden & Pet, each of these components was included and coordinated through an overall center of excellence that supported the ongoing management cadence, communications, measurement, and reinforcement. Other companies have adopted a similar approach. At SunGard Financial Systems, Jim Neve and Ken Powell built a small team focused on sustaining and extending their sales force transformation: "Selling the SunGard Way." Ongoing investment in a capability to sustain your sales force transformation is vital to keep the team from lapsing into old behaviors.

As we discussed in chapter 2 on the levers of sales transformation, organization alignment is a critical success factor for your efforts before, during, and after the transformation. We've seen that many organizations need to complete a full business transformation in addition to the sales force changes to deliver sustained performance improvements that are measured in ways such as increased share of market, profitability, and stock price.

By now, you and your sales force, the key internal players, the external partners, and your company's customers should agree on what's driving the change and how transformation will be implemented. You should all be on the same page of your transformation roadmap with a thorough understanding of how the change will be talked about, reinforced, rewarded, and measured.

While we have yet to find a silver bullet, the steps described in this chapter will increase your odds of sustaining success.

### Chapter 9: Sustaining Your Sales Force Transformation—Takeaways

- The message about sustaining a transformation is no different than sustaining any change, whether it's fitness, strength, or new ways of working.
- Everyone knows that if you stop working out and your diet becomes unhealthy, you will gain weight and lose fitness. Transformation, like physical health, must become a lifestyle and a way of living, or the change will only be fleeting.
- Most successful sales organizations that we've worked with are highly focused on creating a culture of high performance and continuous improvement.
- The sales leaders at these successful organizations continually communicate about discipline, accountability, and performance to get the message to stick. The concept of entropy (the second law of thermodynamics) is instructive here: Entropy is a process in which energy naturally moves from an ordered to a disordered state. In most companies, things

inevitably move from order to chaos if there is not some sort
of control or sustainment process.

- Most successful sales transformations occur in organizations
  with cultures built around standard processes, accountability, and performance management. The lesson regarding sustainment is that if you don't actively adopt at least some of
  the practices and processes described in this chapter, you'll
  revert back to the previous status quo. As we like to tell our
  clients when we're talking about growth: "it's hard to scale
  chaos."

# CHAPTER 10

# Sales Transformations in the Future

Predicting the future is risky—and we don't have a crystal ball showing us future trends and patterns. Over the past several decades, enterprise business-to-business selling has significantly evolved given changes in technology and communications—air travel, fax, pager, mobile phone, the Internet, and social media, among others. Across many industries, this evolution has changed both the balance of knowledge between buyers and sellers and also the expectations buyers have of sellers. Historically, successful salespeople have differentiated themselves by the products and services they offer. But as we've discussed throughout this book, the days of a salesperson adding value by being a talking catalog and product configurator are long gone. Today's top sales professionals, and their customers, leverage the full breadth of technology and communication tools to differentiate themselves and their conversations; a trend that we believe will not only endure but accelerate. As Don Perry told us, "If you take a look at the buyer of the old days and the buyer of today, in the old days sellers used to look for buyers; today buyers are looking for sellers. They research. Their business analysis and access to information have enabled them to get so far down in their buying cycle that the seller of today doesn't look like the seller of yesterday. The buyer has pushed the seller to a level of specialization, and the consequence has changed the dynamics of the sales process. The Internet has made the seller better, and the buyer better."

So, even though you will not find *the* answer to your challenges in this chapter, we do offer several ideas and trends that will shape sales transformations going forward. We divide these trends into the following themes:

- The Rate and Pace of Change is Increasing
- The Internet of Everything
- Experience and Education in Sales
- The Changing Generations in the Workforce
- Personal and Company Brand

Each theme has multiple components that are impacting the sales force and will continue to do so for the foreseeable future. Sales is still very much about human-to-human interactions and relationships, but the nature of communications and data availability has changed the landscape. The genie is out of the bottle—and it's not going back. The smartphone, user-generated content, and social media are not going away anytime soon. The adage that "information wants to be free" has never been more relevant.

## The Rate and Pace of Change is Increasing

Don Perry told us that "sales transformation is like a broken watch. The time is correct only twice a day." Like most things in business, the transformation process is ongoing—witness General Electric's continual transformation for the past 35 years, first under CEO Jack Welch and now under Jeffrey Immelt. Also look at IBM and its well-documented shift from hardware to software to services to analytics and mobility. If the business strategy and product and services are constantly changing, the sales force must change as well.

"One of the most profound changes in the last decade is the dramatic shrinkage of product life cycles which bear little resemblance to the world today which is defined by instant obsolescence," wrote Karsten Horn, director of international sales at INFORM, on the website Sourcingfocus.com. "For example, 50 percent of annual company revenues across a range of industries are derived from new products launched within the past three years. This suggests that long-term product 'cash cows', which stay in a company's portfolio for many years, are becoming a thing of the past."[1] Think about the classic example of Apple in the last decade which has moved from the iMac, to the iPod, iPhone, iPad, and now Apple Watch. What does this mean for the sales force? New products, services, and solutions will come with increasing frequency, which requires an ability to quickly learn and market these solutions and maximize the opportunity before the next "new new thing" arrives.

The pace of change is also reflected in the length of time that workers stay in their job on average: 4.4 years according to the Bureau of Labor Statistics. However, we can expect this rate to accelerate with the new generation of millennials entering the workforce: "Ninety-one percent of Millennials (born between 1977–1997) expect to stay in a job for less than three years,"[2] according to the Future Workplace "Multiple Generations @ Work" survey of 1,189 employees and 150 managers. In other words, these workers should expect to hold 15 to 20 jobs over the course of their careers. In 2014, the research firm CSO Insights found that total turnover in the sales organizations surveyed was 17.1 percent, a historically lower rate based on the lingering effects of the Great Recession in the United States. We expect this rate to increase over the next couple of years, mainly as a result of the tools that help make a more mobile and virtual sales force possible.

## The Internet of Everything

According to a recent study sponsored by data solution experts EMC, "Like the physical universe, the digital universe is large—by 2020 containing nearly as many digital bits as there are stars in the universe. It is doubling in size every two years, and by 2020 the digital universe—the data we create and copy annually—will reach 44 zettabytes, or 44 trillion gigabytes."[3] What will this level of data and analytics bring to your sales force? A challenge is finding insights within the universe of data. A 2014 study by the technology research firm IDC found that in 2013, only 22 percent of the information in the digital universe would be a candidate for analysis, and of that data, IDC estimates that perhaps only 5 percent was especially valuable, or "target rich." IDC predicts that this percentage should more than double by 2020 as enterprises take advantage of new analytics technologies.

The Internet and enabling apps will continue to disrupt the traditional flow of communication from a company to the consumer, which historically relied on either a person doing door-to-door selling or enterprise selling or retail stores to bring products and services to market. In almost every industry, from travel services and hospitality to automobiles, technology, and financial services, what once required many conversations with a person can now be handled online. Twenty years ago, buying an airline ticket, purchasing a stock, booking a hotel reservation, or buying a computer required a personal conversation—either face-to-face or over the phone.

The Internet of things increasingly means automated electronic communications, which in some cases bypass any consumer-vendor interaction. For example, refrigerators are coming that automate inventory control and can automatically order staples, such as milk and eggs, when these run out.

More information will increase the volume of transactional sales. These sales that once required some level of consultation are now almost fully automated. Buying a car or home used to require a significant amount of primary research to determine competitive prices, and in the case of homes, an agent was needed as this information was not publicly available. Today, Zillow, Kelley Blue Book, and other such tools provide real-time information on the value of these assets.

The Internet will increase the amount of data available to buyers/sellers in enterprise/consultative sales. As Don Perry told us, "A new model for the salesperson could be that if [I as a buyer] use the Internet in some shape or form, I could self-serve. It sets up the infrastructure and design for how you might want to be a sales organization in the future. . . . Customers are far too busy to figure out whether they should be talking to you. It's not like the old days. . . . They're in all parts of the world; your access to them is limited. You have to re-think your business in terms of how you are going to operate."

From a sales standpoint, the ability to intelligently and insightfully understand your customer is only going to become more important. In a world of voluminous amounts of data, the ability to sift, sort, and prioritize what's important to the customer's business is paramount. Customers need help in making sense of their issues and understanding how to "cut through the noise" in a sea of data. Many companies are hiring data scientists to help them mine their data and answer some undefined, far-reaching questions. Just as companies need to have a big data plan, so do sales departments. In some ways, we used to have too little data, and now we have too much. The ability to determine what's important and what's not will be the ultimate skill going forward.

Sales teams will benefit from advanced analytics and more focused marketing on the front end. As Chris Donato, a vice president of worldwide sales for HP told us, "In many enterprise sales today, there is a wider group of people to influence, and it is difficult to locate the decision makers. Increasingly, sales professionals will leverage analytical dashboards that will enable greater focus and use of time and resources."

## Experience and Education in Sales

It almost goes without saying, but in a big data world with intelligent buyers sales professionals need to be more analytical and insightful. The need to create deeper levels of differentiation between products and services will only increase. Within one or two clicks, we can often find out what hundreds of customers think of our offerings—the good, the bad, and the ugly. The customer relationship will always be important, but it's an "and," not an "or." You need to bring both personal *and* business value.

As Ken Revenaugh told us, "I believe the complex sale is not going away. Transactional sales may. But complex sales are going to continue to need a human. If we do it right, it becomes a completely different job. At Oakwood, everyone working for me had an MBA—they were one to five years out of their MBAs. At the end of the three years they all wanted to go into sales. At the beginning they wanted to do different things—'I want to be a banker'—but when you see where it's going—top salespeople in good organizations make good money and 'I don't have to slug it out at a desk as an analyst to get there. I could get there in one to three years. I get to bring in products that matter, I get to make a dent in the world, which is what I expected getting out of school!' That was great, seeing a large number of people decide they wanted to be in sales. If we position it right, we could see it attract a lot of talent out of school that weren't attracted years ago." What's more, just a few years ago there was no professional selling training available, but today we have university courses and even four-year degrees in professional selling.

Another key theme we've seen concerns the renewed emphasis on growing your own sales talent. Like a lot of sports teams, you can buy your talent or help cultivate it via farm or academy systems. This idea was echoed by Mike Stankey, the former president of Workday, one of the fastest growing software companies of the past decade:

> The enterprise software space today faces a demographic problem. You take a look at the source of sales hires over the course of the last 20 years, the main body of that sales force has come from the sales academies created by IBM, Xerox, Hewlett-Packard. The companies that recruited great talent out of the universities, put them through intensive classroom and field training programs that lasted a year, and then put them out in the field and gave them great professional selling experience.

> The software companies then swooped in to pick off the best of that talent, which was really the core enterprise sales force for the last 20 years in many businesses... that trained pool of sales talent simply doesn't exist at the rate it did before. Every time these software companies make an acquisition, after the lockup period expires we have hired more people from the acquired companies. But we now find that we have to go outside of the traditional ERP companies to build our sales force.

Mike articulated this talent acquisition strategy in Workday's second-quarter earnings report in 2013. He goes on to describe how Workday screens candidates and then scientifically evaluates them for the key knowledge, skills, and personal characteristics associated with sales success at the organization. While Workday is not hiring candidates without any sales experience, this process is a significant shift from being able to build a sales team from experienced candidates who were trained elsewhere. As Mike summarizes, "So this is very quickly moving to a sales force that is being grown within Workday. And I'm quite pleased to report that the time to first sale is decreasing and the percentage of the sales force that is achieving success is increasing over time. So we believe that this model works. We believe this is a model [that] we'll execute into the future."

At HP, Chris Donato and Larry Stack take a similar approach to bringing on new, relatively inexperienced sales talent, to teach the candidates about enterprise sales while capitalizing on their innate abilities to leverage technologies. These executives are building a new Digital Experience Center that will be staffed with people with less than five years experience and will also present a face of innovation to customers. These executives are modeling the training and team development after the Crossfit® fitness training program. Crossfit® is unlike traditional gyms with weight machines and aerobic classes; instead, it involves intense bursts of activity in a variety of exercises to produce dramatic gains in fitness.

The Crossfit® training and workouts are intense. If you do something wrong, you can get hurt badly. It's the same with sales; you can harm your client or your reputation. As Chris describes the workout, "You show up and want to look like everyone else. So the instructor begins by giving you the basics so you don't hurt yourself. You start to learn one element or motion that you can apply to several exercises and ultimately build five to seven basic motions that you have to do well. We've modeled the training for our new sales center in the same way and focused on basic motions, such as preparing for meeting, identifying a trigger event, handling objections. We want to get the trainees in the environment so they can function and begin to get feedback and learn. We will dedicate some time every day to learning. It's an ongoing and continuous approach." It's an approach that could be disruptive to existing selling models, which excites visionaries such as Chris and Larry.

On occasion, we are invited to speak to undergraduate and graduate business and marketing students. One of our favorite questions to ask is how many of them would like to go into sales when they finish school. How many hands shoot up? You guessed it, maybe one or two out of fifty. When we ask about other professions—management consulting, advertising, digital marketing, or technology—many in the class will enthusiastically raise their hands. Even though selling as a profession has gained more respect and attention as evidenced by the numerous college and university programs focused on professional selling, it still doesn't seem to be an aspirational pursuit for the next generation of college graduates.

However, what's interesting is to ask the same group to consider what happens as you advance in your career in one of the professions we just mentioned. Moving up in a professional services firm to the level of partner indicates that you have certainly mastered a specific domain, but also that you can sell. Of course, no one calls it selling. You hear terms such as "rainmaker," "client partner," "account leader," or "regional leader," but an essential component of the job description is to drive revenue and client relationships. What's clear to us is that a new generation will need to develop advanced selling skills.

## The Changing Generations in the Workforce

The present-day business environment is experiencing a real challenge: four generations are working together at one time. They are sharing office space, sales goals, and widely different opinions about the best strategy for success.

Does anyone hold the power to predict the future of sales transformations? We all know the answer. Still, there are a few facts we can count on for sure, such as the following:

- The age demographics will be greatly affected.
- The average age of decision makers will change.
- Many companies are going to experience change in senior leadership positions due to executives retiring.

- The new crop of sales reps and sales leaders are going to have a different value system than those of the past.
- Doing nothing is not an option in this case.

At this time, 41 percent of the workforce consists of baby boomers (ages 51 to 69). And when you dig a bit deeper, the classification of "later years" of baby boomers should get your attention. Roll the clocks ahead five to ten years and a large portion of these people, with decades of experience, will be on a beach in Florida or somewhere similar. This is the generation that knows no limits to the workweek, is incredibly driven, has an amazing work ethic, and went to the school of hard knocks. Baby boomers have more than left their mark on the workplace. And, well, mathematically speaking, they will soon be gone.

Generation X, which is now 30 percent of the workforce (ages 38 to 50), is finally going to grab many of the senior roles it has been waiting for. These workers are very different from the baby boomers. In general, they are more outspoken and love to be challenged; they're tech-savvy and will work from anywhere, including nontraditional settings.

What does this mean for sales transformations? Let's consider a few impacts for which you should prepare:

- A different age demographic. The millennials and Gen Y will be in many sales roles. These are all people 38 and younger. Depending on your age, you either clapped or shivered. They are wired differently and have different values and require special coaching. Companies will have to be ready to think and act differently in getting the most from this cohort. This new generation did not go to the school of hard knocks and is underwhelmed by the stories of those who did.
- There will be significant changes in sales leadership roles. With many baby boomers leaving, there will be new ideas and new ways of running sales teams. This will cause some growing pains, as the new leaders get comfortable finding the limits of what they can accomplish.

- A heavy influx of millennials and Gen Y in sales roles. We all see this happening already. Some companies have figured out how to train and develop these people, and others are still learning. It is going to take a different approach. Learning will have to be much more dynamic, engaging, and purposeful in order for it to be effective. Gone are the days of long classroom training with this generation.
- Product relevance. We will have to ask ourselves: Who is going to use this product or service? Depending on the answer the functionality will have to be different. There will not be a one-size-fits-all anymore in how products/services are delivered and sold.
- Succession planning. Change is coming on two fronts. First, the baby boomers are going to leave. Second, the millennials and Gen Y will have very little interest in staying at any company for 30 or more years. So, change will be constant, and companies have to be ready to adjust accordingly.
- Hiring "experienced" sellers. This is going to challenge companies greatly. "Experience" comes with a price, and many companies will have to decide if that is worth paying for. This will force many to think about hiring and training some less experienced people who have lower financial demands and different value systems. We may not be hunting these employees with money as the main motivator. It may be other things, such as work environment, team-based selling, the purpose of the company, the ability to make a difference, or the coolness factor of working there. This will stress many companies in many ways.

In the coming years, Gen X will become the old dogs while the millennials and Gen Y groups slowly grow in the roles they either already have or are about to earn. These generations are different in many ways, and it is going to require some new thinking in sales transformations.

### Personal and Company Brand

"As transaction costs in the open market approach zero, so does the size of the firm."[4] This was put forth as the Law of Diminishing Firms by Mui and Downes in one of the seminal books heralding the arrival of e-commerce and the Internet age in 1998. While large firms such as Apple, Disney, and Walmart certainly exist and continue to thrive, advances in technology over the past 20 years have enabled individuals to do more and more—whether as independents or inside large firms. There have always been individuals whose personal reputation either supported or even transcended that of their company—for example, Steve Jobs at Apple, Ted Forstmann at his eponymous firm, or Joe Flom at Skadden Arps. These are high-profile and well-known examples. What's interesting is that social technologies such as websites, blogs, LinkedIn®, Twitter®, and others have enabled new ways to establish expertise and build a personal brand.

We have worked with and profiled many rainmakers (see http://symmetricsgroup.com/top-performers/ for some examples) in industries such as law, investments, software sales, management consulting, real estate, and even automobile sales. Each of these individuals has built up a powerful personal brand over time. Johnny Van is a great example. Most people view car sales as transactional, but Johnny Van sees it as relational. Honesty, reliability, and integrity are his hallmarks. If a customer can get a better deal elsewhere, Johnny will tell the customer to go for it. "Everyone has been hurt somehow buying a car," he says. "Or they have heard a horror story. People bring that baggage to the sale, and you have to recognize it while trying to make them comfortable."[5]

Over a 38-year career, Johnny has turned follow-up into an art form. Along the way, he's become an institution in western New York. Each year, Johnny makes about 10,000 "birthday calls" to clients. "It's a good time to find out what's good with the family and their cars," he says. "I check contact info and I update files—who got married, who moved." Along the way, there have been obstacles. Car buyers traded in more often when warranties ran out after just one year. Today, cars are built to last longer. Still, Johnny Van works his system, following up diligently with every customer. And from those follow-ups come the qualified leads that can make or break a sales

**Table 10.1** Future Trends Applied to the Way of Sales

| | Current | Future |
|---|---|---|
| **Strategy & Structure** | • Product lifespan of 5–10 years<br>• Market and customer segmentation strategy revisited on an annual basis<br>• Strategy developed from the inside out with little involvement of customers or channel partners | • Quicker iterations of strategies with faster product lifecycles<br>• Segmentation that includes social, persona, and more predictive analytics and is constantly refreshed<br>• More use of virtual teams, inside sales, and pools of experts<br>• Collaborative ecosystem with partners, suppliers, and customers involved in cocreation |
| **Processes & Tools** | • Prescriptive Sales Process based on linear execution of the sales stages<br>• Packaged sales methodologies still encourage a "silver bullet" mentality | • Greater focus on dynamic processes with real-time feedback from the customer data stream<br>• Smarter account and territory management processes – infused with data from the customer and market<br>• CRMs that are more intelligent in terms of helping to select analogous opportunities and the next best offer or conversation |
| **Enablement & People** | • Salespeople are trained and reviewed in a linear sales process<br>• Compensation is variable and aligned with short-term business objectives, ensuring the seller will take the easiest and quickest route possible to any type of revenue | • A focus on analytical and synthesis skills given the vast amounts of data<br>• Talent management focus on developing the right skills vs. buying them.<br>• Greater focus on developing foundational selling skills that allow adaptation<br>• More insight-focused and more consultative about testing the customer's assumptions—a problem-solving "partner" |
| **Metrics & Management** | • Reports and metrics driven from CRM systems with a reliance on "lagging" indicators | • Greater use of predictive analytics to inform future behaviors and structures<br>• Smarter dashboards that help to proactively alert when metrics are outside of desired bands<br>• Great focus on real-time coaching and communications |

career. "I don't have hobbies," notes Johnny. "My hobby has always been the sales game. A new guy sells 1 or 3 out of 10 customers. I sell 8 out of 10. This is my golf game." Like a baseball fan who can reel off batting averages as far back as 1964, Johnny Van can tell you how many cars he sold in a given month decades ago. He's like a living, breathing CRM system.

### Chapter 10: Sales Force Transformations in the Future—Takeaways

- While there are no sure-bet predictions for the future of sales transformations, we categorize the trends into five key themes:
  - *The Rate and Pace of Change is Increasing*—Transformation is ongoing. If the business strategy and product and services are constantly changing, the sales force must change as well.
  - *The Internet of Everything*—The Internet and enabling apps will continue to disrupt the traditional flow of communication from sellers to consumers.
  - *Experience and Education in Sales*—In today's big data world, sales professionals need to be more analytical and insightful. They must create deeper levels of differentiation. The good news is that while just a few years ago, there were virtually no college classes on how to sell, today, there are four-year programs on this. Seek new ways to train and motivate your Gen X and millennial salespeople. Remember, they didn't attend the school of hard knocks, and they're generally unimpressed by the "war stories" of those who did.
- *The Changing Generations in the Workforce*—Today, four generations comprise the workforce. Each has different values, different motivators, and a different approach to selling.

- *Personal and Company Brand*—Even as technology and social networks gain a greater influence on the buying process, we've seen individual salespeople—rainmakers—work hard to establish their personal brand to differentiate themselves and their products and services.
  - Using our four-tiered approach to the Way of Sales discussed in chapter 5, we recommend a way forward with sales force transformations aimed at quicker strategy implementation, market segmentation, more focus on dynamic processes, smarter territory management and CRM use, more emphasis on the analytical aspects of selling, and more reliance on predictive analytics.

# Notes

## 1 The Transformation Dilemma

1. Chandru Krishnamurthy, Juliet Johansson, and Hank Schlissberg. "Solutions Selling: Is the Pain Worth the Gain?" *McKinsey Quarterly*, 2003, http://insightdemand.com/wp-content/uploads/2011/10/MckinseySolutionSelling.pdf>.
2. Lawrence B. Chonko, James A. Roberts, and Eli Jones, "Diagnosing Sales Force Change Resistance: What We Can Learn From the Addiction Literature," *Marketing Management Journal* 16, no. 1 (Spring 2006): 44–71.
3. Thomas J. Peters and Robert H. Waterman, Jr., *In Search of Excellence: Lessons from America's Best-Run Companies* (New York: Warner Books, 1982).
4. Jim Collins and Jerry I. Porras, *Built to Last: Successful Habits of Visionary Companies* (HarperBusiness, 1997).
5. Jim Collins, *Good to Great: Why Some Companies Make the Leap...And Others Don't* (HarberBusiness, 2001).
6. Frank Cespedes, *Aligning Strategy and Sales: The Choice, Systems, and Behaviors that Drive Effective Selling* (Harvard Business Review Press, 2014), 29.
7. Cynthia Sass, "5 Reasons Most Diets Fail Within 7 Days," September 19, 2013. Retrieved September 20, 2015, from http://news.health.com/2013/09/19/5-reasons-most-diets-fail-within-7-days/.
8. Matthew Dixon and Brent Adamson, *The Challenger Sale: Taking Control of the Customer Conversation.* (Portfolio, 2011).
9. Brent Adamson, Matthew Dixon, and Nicholas Toman, "The End of Solution Sales," *Harvard Business Review,* July–August, 2012.

## 2 The Levers of Sales Transformation

1. Eric Schmidt and Jonathan Rosenberg, *How Google Works* (Grand Central Publishing, 2014), 11.
2. Jim Collins, *Good to Great: Why Some Companies Make the Leap...And Others Don't* (HarberBusiness, 2001).

## 3 Building the Foundation and Vision of the Future

1. Daryl Connor, *Managing at the Speed of Change* (Random House, 1993), 93–94.
2. Michael Watkins, *The First 90 Days* (Harvard Business School Press, 2003).

3. Shawn Lankton and Brian Stafford, "B2B Sales Is Being Massively Disrupted (Hint: It's Looking More Like B2C)," October 13, 2015. Retrieved September 20, 2015, from http://www.forbes.com/sites/mckinsey/2013/10/15/sales-disruption-eruption-b2b-sales-go-consumer/.

4. Voltaire, *Project Gutenberg's Voltaire's Philosophical Dictionary* (http://www.gutenberg.org/files/18569/18569-h/18569-h.htm), 78.

5. John DeVincentis and Neil Rackham, *Rethinking the Sales Force* (McGraw-Hill Education, 1999).

## 5 Building Your Sales Transformation Roadmap

1. James C. Collins, *Good to Great: Why Some Companies Make the Leap—and Others Don't* (New York, NY: HarperBusiness, 2001), 13.

2. Jeroen de Flander, "Home page: about," retrieved Septempber 19, 2015, from http://jeroen-de-flander.com/about/Sep 13, 2015.

3. Phil Wahba, "Amazon Gets Needed Boost in 2014 from Outside Sellers," retrieved September 19, 2015, from http://fortune.com/2015/01/05/amazon-third-party-sellers/.

## 6 Implementing Your Sales Transformation

1. Marshall Goldsmith and Mark Reiter, *What Got You Here Won't Get You There: How Successful People Become Even More Successful* (Hachette Books, 2007).

## 7 Key Barriers and Considerations for Implementation

1. Jim Collins, *Good to Great: Why Some Companies Make the Leap...And Others Don't* (Harper Business, 2001), 1.

2. http://www.nytimes.com/2015/05/03/upshot/andreessen-horowitz-dealmaker-to-the-stars-of-silicon-valley.html?abt=0002&abg=1.

3. Donald Sull, Rebecca Homkes, and Charles Sull, "Why Strategy Execution Unravels—and What to Do About It," *Harvard Business Review*, March 2015.

4. Donald Daly, "What Motivates a Salesperson – The Results Are in!" March, 14 2010; retrieved September 19, 2015, from http://blog.thetasgroup.com/donals-blog/what-motivates-a-salesperson-the-results-are-in.

5. Towers Watson, "For Optimal Sales Force Performance, Pay Is Not Enough," *Perspectives*, June 18, 2013. Retrieved September 19, 2015, from https://www.towerswatson.com/en-US/Insights/IC-Types/Ad-hoc-Point-of-View/Perspectives/2013/For-Optimal-Sales-Force-Performance-Pay-Is-Not-Enough.

## 8 Extending Your Sales Transformation to Business Partners, Suppliers, and Customers

1. Patricia E. Moody and Rick B. Mayo, "Supplier Relationships Key to Honda's Healthy Profit Margins," May 23, 2012. Retrieved September 19, 2015, from http://www.industryweek.com/blog/supplier-relationships-key-hondas-healthy-profit-margins.

2. Taleris website, "About Us," retrieved September 19, 2015, from http://www.taleris.com/about.html.

3. Carsten Baumgarth and Las Binckebanck, "Sales Force Impact on B-to-B Brand Equity: Conceptual Framework and Empirical Test," *Journal of Product & Brand Management*, 20 (2011): 487–98.

4. Peter F. Drucker, *The Practice of Management* (New York: Harper & Row, 1954), 37.

## 9   Sustaining Your Sales Transformation

1. Alex O'Meara, "The Percentage of People Who Regain Weight After Rapid Weight Loss and the Risks of Doing So." Retrieved November 2, 2015, from http://www.livestrong.com/article/438395-the-percentage-of-people-who-regain-weight-after-rapid-weight-loss-risks/.

2. Teo K., Lear S., Islam S., et al. "Prevalence of a Healthy Lifestyle Among Individuals With Cardiovascular Disease in High-, Middle- and Low-Income Countries: The Prospective Urban Rural Epidemiology (PURE) Study." *JAMA* 309(15) (2013): 1613–1621. doi:10.1001/jama.2013.3519.

3. http://www.today.com/id/42936158/ns/today-today_health/t/tips-make-fitness-last-lifetime/.

4. Carolyn Aiken, Dmitriy Galper, Scott Keller, "Winning Hearts and Minds: The Secrets to Sustaining Change," *Lead Management: New Frontiers for Financial Institutions* (McKinsey, 2011), 46–53.

5. Jim Collins, *Good to Great: Why Some Companies Make the Leap...And Others Don't* (Harper Business, 2001).

6. Jim Collins, *How The Mighty Fall: And Why Some Companies Never Give In* (Harper Business, 2009).

7. Christopher McDougall. *Born to Run: A Hidden Tribe, Superathletes, and the Greatest Race the World Has Never Seen* (New York: Knopf, 2009), 13.

8. George Labovitz and Victor Rosansky, *The Power of Alignment: How Great Companies Stay Centered and Accomplish Extraordinary Things* (New York: Wiley, 1997), 3.

9. Stephanie Baker and Katya Kazakina. "Auction Wars: Christie's, Sotheby's, and The Art of Competition," June 21, 2015. Retrieved September 20, 2015, from http://www.bloomberg.com/news/articles/2015-06-21/auction-wars-christie-s-sotheby-s-and-the-art-of-competition.

10. Ibid.

11. Michael Hammer and James Champy, *Reengineering the Corporation: A Manifesto for Business Revolution* (Harper Business, 2006).

## 10   Sales Transformations in the Future

1. Karsten Horn, "The Product Life Cycle is in Decline," retrieved September 20, 2015, from http://www.sourcingfocus.com/site/opinionscomments/the_product_life_cycle_is_in_decline/.

2. Jeanne Meister, "Job Hopping Is the 'New Normal' for Millennials: Three Ways to Prevent a Human Resource Nightmare," August 14, 2012. Retrieved September 20, 2015, from http://www.forbes.com/sites/jeannemeister/2012/08/14/job-hopping-is-the-new-normal-for-millennials-three-ways-to-prevent-a-human-resource-nightmare/.

3. http://www.emc.com/leadership/digital-universe/2014iview/executive-summary.htm.

4. Larry Downes and Chunka Mui, *Unleashing the Killer App* (Cambridge: Harvard Business School Press, 1998), 32.

5. Personal communication (via interview) with Johnny Van. November 9, 2011.

# Index